Nova
Zembla

Tartara

Norvegia

Tangut

Mo

Suedia

Bergen

Cattigara

Negrod

Wilki

Calami

Cossin

S.Nicolao

Tartaria

Gruslua

Turfon

Campi

en

Carthaio

Russia

Marno

rea

Cotan

Singui

Geuza

EVROPA

Cigai

Balaar

ASIA

Casbin

Mossens

Congu

Quansu

Gallia

Buda

Turcheltan

Voci

Iaci

China

Miao

Armenia

Samarchand

am

La

Natolia

Coralan

Ama

Caeis

Soria

Persia

Turbat

Candahar

Cranche

Mian

Liangui

Loqno

Barba

ria.

Guzarate

India orien

talis

Lichi

Aegyptus

Mar

Can

Deuan

AFRICA

Arabia

Orixa

Brema

Agi

Canu

Nubia

Fartach

Goa

Caplos

Malaca

Pulo

 Palohan

Hiam

na

lymba

Aden

Calecuta

Man

bay

Abillini

Magadaxo

Zeilan

Iaua

Manicongo

Vaso de Acuna

Gylam

Manf

Melinde

S.Francesco

Due Compagne

Iana rea

OCEANVS AE

Adare

Don Garcia

Poueada

THIOPICVS

Lion

fona

Lanchido

S.Helena

Batos de Nazares

Mascarenhas

Apollonia

MAR DI INDI

LYOA

Tristan de

Acuna

Iuan de

Lisboa

MALETVR

Gonsalo Aluares

C.Bone spes

Las Romeras

Vastissimas hic esse

regiones ex M.Pauli Ven: et

Lud.Vartomani scriptis pe

regrinationibus constat.

Psitacorum regio,

sic a Lusitanis appellata ob in

credibile earum auium harum

magnitudinem.

30 40 50 60 70 80 90 100 110 120 130 140 150 160 170 180

S NONDVM COGNITA

People Together

ADVENTURES IN TIME AND PLACE

James A. Banks

Barry K. Beyer

Gloria Contreras

Jean Craven

Gloria Ladson-Billings

Mary A. McFarland

Walter C. Parker

NATIONAL
GEOGRAPHIC
SOCIETY

THIS STORYTELLER DOLL WAS
MADE BY A PUEBLO ARTIST.
LISTENING TO STORIES IS ONE
WAY TO LEARN ABOUT THE PAST.

THE
PRINCETON
REVIEW

**McGraw-Hill
School Division**

New York   Farmington

PROGRAM AUTHORS

Dr. James A. Banks
Professor of Education and
Director of the Center for
Multicultural Education
University of Washington
Seattle, Washington

Dr. Barry K. Beyer
Professor Emeritus, Graduate
School of Education
George Mason University
Fairfax, Virginia

Dr. Gloria Contreras
Professor of Education
University of North Texas
Denton, Texas

Jean Craven
District Coordinator of
Curriculum Development
Albuquerque Public Schools
Albuquerque, New Mexico

Dr. Gloria Ladson-Billings
Professor of Education
University of Wisconsin
Madison, Wisconsin

Dr. Mary A. McFarland
Instructional Coordinator of
Social Studies, K–12, and
Director of Staff Development
Parkway School District
Chesterfield, Missouri

Dr. Walter C. Parker
Professor and Program Chair for
Social Studies Education
University of Washington
Seattle, Washington

**NATIONAL
GEOGRAPHIC
SOCIETY**
Washington, D.C.

CONSULTANTS FOR
TEST PREPARATION

THE
PRINCETON
REVIEW

The Princeton Review is not affiliated
with Princeton University or ETS.

CALIFORNIA SENIOR
CONSULTANT

Dr. Carlos E. Cortés
Professor Emeritus of History
University of California
Riverside, California

CALIFORNIA PROGRAM
CONSULTANTS

Diane Bowers
Former Assistant Director of Education
for the Yurok Tribe
Klamath, California

Dr. Susan L. Douglass
Affiliated Scholar, Council on Islamic
Education
Fountain Valley, California

Dr. Karen Nakai
Lecturer of History-Social Science
Department of Education
University of California
Irvine, California

Shelly Osborne
Teacher-Literacy Mentor
Franklin School
Alameda, California

Dr. Valerie Ooka Pang
Professor, School of Teacher Education
San Diego State University
San Diego, California

Lyn Reese
Director, Women in History Project
Berkeley, California

Dr. Curtis C. Roseman
Professor of Geography
University Of Southern California
Los Angeles, California

Dr. Robert M. Senkewicz
Professor of History
Santa Clara University
Santa Clara, California

Evelyn Staton
Librarian
San Francisco School District
Member, Multiethnic Literature Forum
for San Francisco
San Francisco, California

Dr. Clifford E. Trafzer
Department of Ethnic Studies
University of California
Riverside, California

PROGRAM CONSULTANTS

Dr. John Bodnar
Professor of History
Indiana University
Bloomington, Indiana

Dr. Sheilah Clark-Ekong
Professor, Department of Anthropology
University of Missouri, St. Louis
St. Louis, Missouri

Dr. Darlene Clark Hine
John A. Hannah Professor of History
Michigan State University
East Lansing, Michigan

Dr. John L. Esposito
Professor of Religion and
International Affairs
Georgetown University
Washington, D. C.

Dr. Gary Manson
Department of Geography
Michigan State University
East Lansing, Michigan

Dr. Juan Mora-Torrés
Professor of Latin American History
University of Texas at San Antonio
San Antonio, Texas

Dr. Joseph Rosenbloom
Professor, Classics Department
Washington University
St. Louis, Missouri

Dr. Robert Seltzer
Professor of Jewish History
Hunter College
City University of New York

Dr. Peter Stearns
Dean, College of Humanities
and Social Studies
Carnegie Mellon University
Pittsburgh, Pennsylvania

CONSULTING AUTHORS

Dr. James Flood
Professor of Teacher Education, Reading
and Language Development
San Diego State University
San Diego, California

Dr. Diane Lapp
Professor of Teacher Education, Reading
and Language Development
San Diego State University
San Diego, California

GRADE-LEVEL
CONSULTANTS

Bertha Addison
Second Grade Teacher
Maxwell Park Elementary School
Oakland, California

Ava Parker Bevins
Second Grade Teacher
Bradley Creek School
Wilmington, North Carolina

Olga Briseño
Elementary School Teacher
Grant Elementary School
San Jose, California

Hilda Magana
Second Grade Teacher
Nestor Elementary School
San Diego, California

Shellye Perez
Second Grade Teacher
Martin Luther King, Jr.,
Elementary School
Santa Anna, California

Carol Peterson
Second Grade Teacher
LeClaire Elementary School
Edwardsville, Illinois

Janet Rhodes
Elementary School Teacher
Crestwood Elementary School
Crestwood, Missouri

Jo Nell Rogers
Second Grade Teacher
Stephens Elementary School
Houston, Texas

Cheryl R. Zakrzewski
Second Grade Teacher
Elias Howe School
Bridgeport, Connecticut

CONTRIBUTING
WRITERS

Linda Ward Beech
New York, New York

Linda Scher
Raleigh, North Carolina

Acknowledgments

The publisher gratefully acknowledges permission to reprint the following material:

"Relatives" from **The Butterfly Jar** by Jeff Moss. Copyright © 1989 by Jeff
Moss. Used by permission of Bantam Books, a division of Bantam
Doubleday Dell Publishing Group, Inc.
From **This is My House** by Arthur Dorros. Copyright © 1992 by Arthur
Dorros. Scholastic, Inc.
Text from "My Mami Takes Me To The Bakery" from **The Tamarindo
Puppy** by Charlotte Pomerantz. © 1980 by Charlotte Pomerantz. Green-
willow Books, a division of William Morrow & Company, Inc.

"The Stars and Stripes Forever" by John Philip Sousa, adapted by Teresa
Jennings. © 1991 by Plank Road Publishing, Inc. All Rights Reserved.
How My Family Lives in America Reprinted with the permission of
Simon & Schuster Books for Young Readers from HOW MY FAMILY LIVES
IN AMERICA by Susan Kuklin. Copyright 1992 Susan Kuklin.
"This Land is Your Land" Words and Music by Woody Guthrie. ©
copyright 1956 (Renewed) and 1958 (Renewed) 1970 Ludlow Music, Inc.,
New York City, New York. (continued on page R20)

McGraw-Hill School Division

*A Division of The **McGraw·Hill** Companies*

McGraw-Hill School Division
Two Penn Plaza
New York, New York 10121

Printed in the United States of America

ISBN 0-02-148822-3

2 3 4 5 6 7 8 9 004 03 02 01 00 99

CONTENTS

UNIT ONE
2

Family Ties

UNIT TWO
38

Earth, Our Home

UNIT THREE A Working World
80

UNIT FOUR We the People
116

People, Places, and Holidays

REFERENCE SECTION

STANDARDIZED TEST SUPPORT

THE PRINCETON REVIEW

FEATURES

MANY VOICES

CHARTS & GRAPHS

MAPS

YOUR TEXTBOOK at a glance

Your book is called *People Together: Adventures in Time and Place*. It has many parts.

NATIONAL GEOGRAPHIC
Look at Your World

How do products get from factories to stores?

What does this place have that other places don't have?

One special part of your book is called **Look at Your World**. It shows places in our country.

LESSON 1

Let's go!

A Trip to the Market

Ann and her parents live in the city of San Francisco. This city is in the state of California. They are shopping at an outdoor market.

This market is a busy place. Many people come here to sell things. Others come here to buy things. Ann looks at the different goods that are for sale. Goods are things that people make or grow.

Ann helps her parents to pick out some corn. They will have corn with dinner tonight.

82

Your book has six units. Each unit has many lessons. You will learn new things in each lesson.

Some units Close with a Story. Others close with a poem or a song.

CLOSE With A Story

from How My Family Lives in America

My papa came to New York without his parents to go to school and my mama moved here with her family.

THINKING SKILLS
Finding Alike and Different

Things can be alike and different. Things that are alike are the same in some way. Things that are different are not the same in some way.

Jane's family receives holiday cards from relatives every year. Look at the cards below. The card on the left was sent two years ago. It shows Jane's Aunt Carol, Uncle John, cousin Andrew, and cousin Cathy.

177

CITIZENSHIP
Making a Difference

Some people in Nashville gave the group a big field for the first Kid's Yard. There they planted trees, bushes, and flowers. "As the plants grow," Melissa said, "their berries and leaves will bring birds, butterflies, and bugs. Animals will come, and birds will build nests for their babies."

Melissa is spreading her ideas. A business helped her print many posters for the group. The posters tell how to start a Kid's Yard. Melissa sends them to schools and groups. She also sends them to anyone who writes to her. "Trees, animals, and people all need each other," she said. "We can all help planet Earth."

13

65

San Francisco
CALIFORNIA

Ann stops by the bread stand. "May I pick out some bread?" Ann asks her mother. "It smells so good!"

At the next stand Ann's father sees some strawberry jam. "This is my favorite kind," he says. "We can put it on the bread."

That looks good!

83

Some special lessons tell about people who are Making a Difference. Others tell about **Making Choices.**

PICTURE GLOSSARY

Dictionary of GEOGRAPHIC WORDS

HILL Land that is higher than the land around it, but lower than a mountain.

PENINSULA Land that has water on three sides.

PLAIN Flat land.

LAKE Body of water with land all around it.

OREGON

Look at the back of your book. The Dictionary of Geographic Words and Picture Glossary tell what words mean.

Look at Your World

How do products get from factories to stores?

What does this place have that other places don't have?

What is this place like in the winter?

What do people grow on farms?

How do people find their way around?

4TH
ST
400

GEOGRAPHY SKILLS
Using Maps

What is a map?

A map is a drawing of a place. Look at the picture of the neighborhood. The picture shows what the neighborhood looks like from above. The map on the next page is a drawing of the same neighborhood. How are the map and the picture alike?

What is a symbol?

Many maps have symbols. A symbol is something that stands for something else. Symbols on a map may be shapes, colors, or pictures. What symbols do you see on this map?

What is a map key?

A map key tells what the symbols on a map mean. Find the map key. What symbol stands for a pool? How many symbols are on the map key?

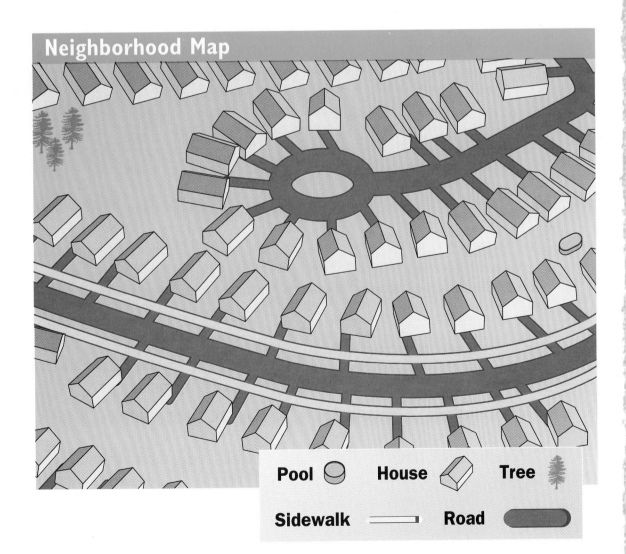

Neighborhood Map

Pool ⬭	House ▱	Tree 🌲
Sidewalk ▭	Road ▬	

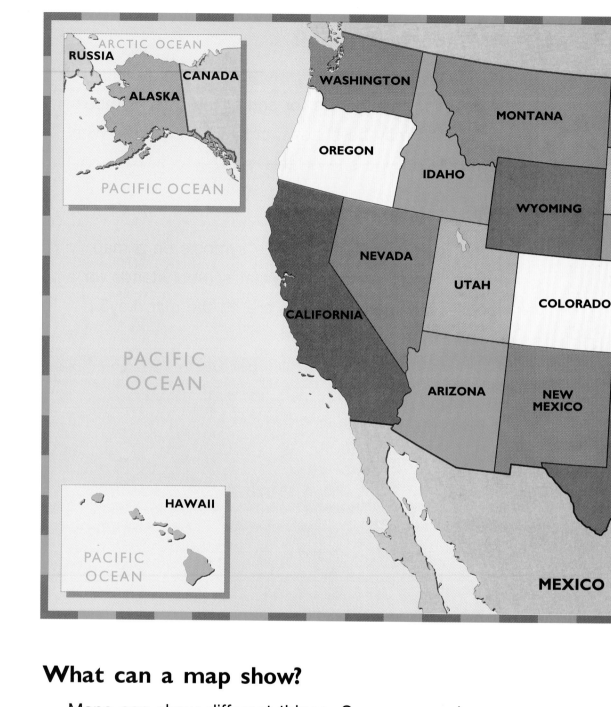

What can a map show?

Maps can show different things. Some maps show neighborhoods or cities. Some show land and water.

Most maps have a title. The title tells you what the map shows. What is the title of this map?

THE UNITED STATES

This is a map of the United States. The United States is a **country**. A country is a land and the people who live there.

Some maps show **states**. A state is a part of a country. The United States is made up of 50 states. What is the name of your state? Find it on the map. Name a state that looks bigger than your state.

Using Globes

How is a globe like Earth?

Earth is round, like a ball. It is made up of land and water. A globe is a model of Earth. A model is a small copy of something. Sometimes a globe uses blue to show water. It uses other colors to show land. What ways are Earth and a globe alike?

What are continents and oceans?

Earth has seven continents. Continents are very large bodies of land. Which continents do you see on this globe?

Earth also has four very large bodies of salt water. They are called oceans. Which oceans do you see on this globe?

Earth

North Pole

UNITED STATES

PACIFIC OCEAN

ATLANTIC OCEAN

SOUTH AMERICA

BRAZIL

South Pole

A Globe

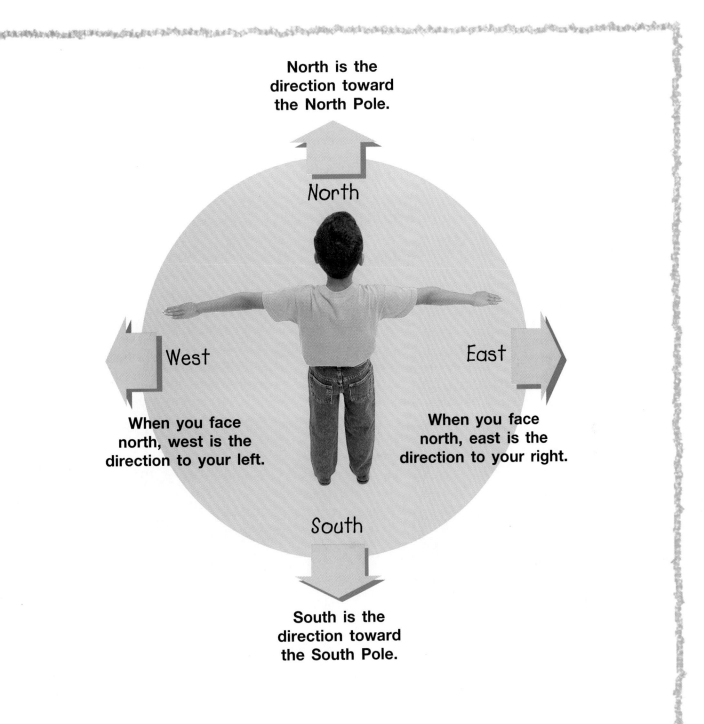

North is the
direction toward
the North Pole.

North

West

When you face
north, west is the
direction to your left.

East

When you face
north, east is the
direction to your right.

South

South is the
direction toward
the South Pole.

What are directions?

There are four main directions. The directions
are north, east, south, and west.

Directions can help you find things on globes and
maps. Which ocean is west of North America? Which
continent is south of North America?

Key Words

history

tradition

relative

ancestor

neighborhood

community

suburb

transportation

UNIT ONE

Family Ties

Family Clues

The students in Mrs. Brandon's Grade 2 class are looking for clues. They are looking for clues to learn about their family **history**. History is the story of the past.

"Your job is to find out things you do today that your family members did in the past," says Mrs. Brandon. "These ways of doing things are called **traditions**. A tradition is a special way of doing something that was passed down over time."

Family Treasures

ROBERT

"Members of my family get to use a special plate on their birthdays," says Jane. "My grandmother did the same thing with my mother. My mother says that the tradition helps her to remember her family history."

Mom, age 7

Robert found out that his name is a tradition. "My name was passed down from my grandfather to my father. Then it was passed down to me," says Robert. "I am the third Robert in my family!"

Jack found out that he and his father share a tradition. "Every Spring we fly a kite," says Jack. "This is a tradition passed down to my dad from his father."

Linda knows a special folk dance called "los viejitos." It is a tradition her grandfather taught her. "He learned the dance when he was a boy," says Linda.

Tara's favorite animal is the coyote. She learned that telling stories about them is one of her family traditions. "In some stories, Coyote plays tricks. In others, he makes things and helps people," says Tara.

1. What are traditions?

2. What traditions are part of your family history or a family you know?

Great-Grandpa Lang

Great-Grandma Lang

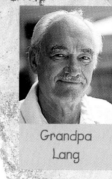
Great-Grandpa McGill

Great-Grandma McGill

Grandpa Lang

Grandma Lang

My Dad

My Brother

A Family Tree

"A family tree shows your **relatives**," says Jane. "A relative is a person who belongs to the same family as someone else."

"This is my family tree," says Jane. "The left side shows relatives of my dad. Relatives of my mom are on the right. Everyone on the family tree is related to me! But only my mom, my brother, and I live together."

8

Great-Grandpa
Manning

Great-Grandma
Manning

Great-Grandpa
Westcott

Great-Grandma
Westcott

Grandpa
Manning

Grandma
Manning

My Mom

Family trees show a family's history. "My family tree shows some of my **ancestors**," says Jane. "Ancestors are relatives who lived before you were born."

Me

9

Grandma Lang's flower shop

Every person's family tree is different. Not all people know about their relatives and ancestors. Finding out about ancestors can be hard.

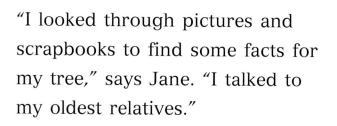

"I looked through pictures and scrapbooks to find some facts for my tree," says Jane. "I talked to my oldest relatives."

Grandpa Manning and me as a baby

"I also found out that my family is much bigger than I thought," says Jane. "I have lots of aunts, uncles, and cousins. They are my relatives, too!"

My Mom, my brother, and me

My aunts, uncles, and cousins at the family reunion

1. What can a family tree show?

2. How might you learn about your family or a family you know?

THINKING SKILLS
Finding Alike and Different

Things can be **alike** and **different**. Things that are alike are the same in some way. Things that are different are not the same in some way.

Jane's family receives holiday cards from relatives every year. Look at the cards below. The card on the left was sent two years ago. It shows Jane's Aunt Carol, Uncle John, cousin Andrew, and cousin Cathy.

The card on the right is this year's card. It is like the first card because it shows the same family. But it is different because it shows Jane's new baby cousin Ruth. What else is the same about each card? What else is different?

Happy Holidays!

Love,
Carol, John, Andrew, and Cathy

Season's Greetings

Love,
Carol, John, Andrew, Cathy, and Ruth

Trying the Skill

These pictures show two houses where Robert's uncle lived. The top picture shows the first house he lived in. The bottom picture shows the house Robert's uncle lives in today.

1. Tell how the pictures of the houses are alike.

2. Tell how they are different.

3. Think about the rooms in your school. How are they alike? How are they different?

Where We Lived

Every family has a different history. Robert made a book to show the places his family has lived over time. These are part of his family's special history.

Places We Have Lived

I lived here.

Buster

This house was in the state of Georgia. It is where I lived until I was five. That was the year I got Buster, my dog.

Homes are part of a **neighborhood**. A neighborhood is a place where people live, work, and play. James and Laura lived near me. They were my neighbors. We had fun together.

James

James's house

Laura's house

Laura

My School

Main Street

Carnesville

GEORGIA

Neighborhoods make up a **community**. A community has many different neighborhoods.

Communities can be large or small. A small community is a town. Our town's name was Carnesville. There are many places to see and things to do in Carnesville.

Not far from Carnesville are farms and open countryside. Every summer I lived with my Grandma and Grandpa on their farm. They grow and sell vegetables and peaches. People from all over the state come to the farm to buy Grandma's peach pie.

Grandma and Grandpa's peach trees

We moved to San Mateo.

When I was five, my mom got a new job. We moved to San Mateo. San Mateo is a **suburb** in the state of California. A suburb is a community just outside of a city. A city is a large community with many people.

When I was six, we moved from the suburbs into the city. We moved into the city of San Francisco. Now we live in an apartment building.

We've moved again.

Some families live in the same place for a long time. Other families move often. Wherever you live, that place is part of your family's history.

1. Is your community in a city, town, or in the countryside? How can you tell?

2. What kinds of places are in your family history?

On the Go, Then and Now

Families use different kinds of **transportation**. Transportation is a way of moving people or goods from one place to another. "My family uses bikes and a car to get around," says Jack. "Sometimes we use a bus. Airplanes and trains help us to travel to faraway places quickly."

Transportation has changed over time. In the past some families used horses and wagons to get around. Often it took months for families to reach where they wanted to go.

My Family

"Transportation can be part of a family's history," says Jack. "My great-great grandfather came to the United States from the country of China on a ship. He helped lay tracks for the first railroad to go across the continent of North America. Then families could travel across our country by train."

Railroad Workers

1. What kinds of transportation do you use?

2. How is transportation part of your family's history?

21

STUDY SKILLS
Using Calendars

A **calendar** is a chart that shows the months of the year. Each year has 12 months. A calendar also shows how many days are in each month. It also names the days of the week.

September

Sunday	Monday	Tuesday	Wednesday	Thursday	Friday	Saturday
			1	2	3	4
5	Labor Day 6	School Starts 7	8	9	10	Visit Grandma 11
12	13	14	15	16	17	Soccer 18
19	20	21	Class Trip 22	23	24	Soccer 25
26	27	28	29	30		

Jack uses his calendar to mark family trips, things he does at school, and other important days.

Look at Jack's calendar for September. Find the number 7. On what day of the week is September 7? What happened on September 7?

October

Sunday	Monday	Tuesday	Wednesday	Thursday	Friday	Saturday
					1	2
3	Grandma Gloria's Birthday 4	5	6	7	8	9
10	11	Columbus Day 12	13	14	Grandma Maria's Birthday 15	16
17	18	19	20	21	22	23
24 / 31	25	26	27	28	29	30

Trying the Skill

Answer the questions below about Linda's calendar for the month of October.

1. How many days are in this month?

2. What happened on October 4?

3. How many days was it from Grandma Gloria's birthday to Grandma Maria's birthday?

4. On what day of the week was Grandma Maria's birthday?

5. How do you use calendars in school? How do you use calendars at home?

23

Where We Came From

Linda, her sister, and her brother were born in the United States. So were her parents and her grandparents. They are Americans. "We are also Mexican Americans," says Linda. "That means that one or more of our ancestors came from the country of Mexico. In Mexico people speak Spanish."

Mis Bisabuelos
(My Great-Grandparents)

My great-grandparents lived in Mexico long ago. They owned a small farm in the town of Zamora. On their farm they grew avocados, corn, sugarcane, and mangos. They sold their crops at the market in the town square.

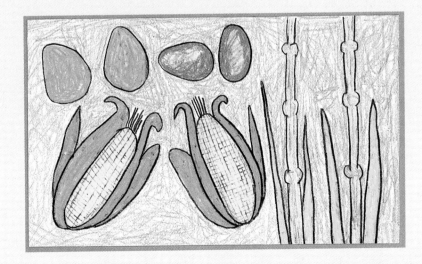

My great-grandparents lived in Zamora until a war broke out. Like many other Mexican families during that time, they moved to the United States. They made the journey by train and by bus.

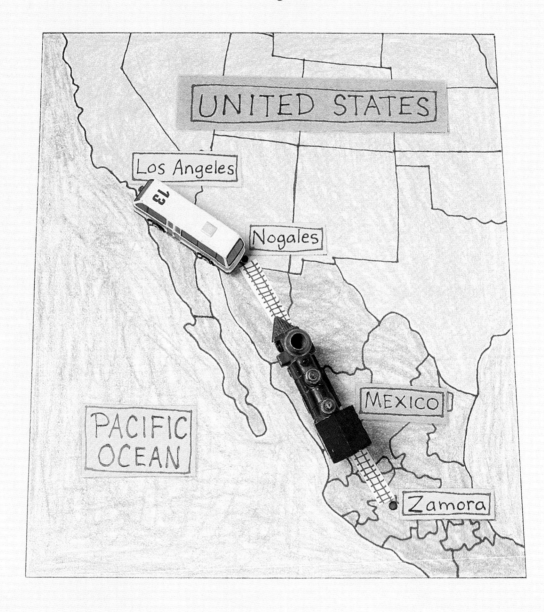

Mis Abuelo
(My Grandfather)

In 1920 they moved to Los Angeles. That is a city in California. My great-grandfather took a job on a farm nearby. Soon after that, my grandfather was born.

I learned this story and many Mexican traditions from my grandfather. He also taught me to speak Spanish like my ancestors!

El Fin

That means "The End" in Spanish.

1. **What did Linda learn from her grandfather?**

2. **From what country or countries might the ancestors of your family or a family you know have come?**

Treasures from the Past

Tara is a Native American. The ancestors of Native Americans were the first people to live in America. Tara belongs to a group of Native Americans called Pomo. Today, many Pomo live in California.

One day, Tara found a very old woven basket at her grandmother's house. "Who made this basket?" Tara asks.

"Your great-great grandmother made it," Grandmother says. "It is a link to our past. The Pomo still make these baskets. You can make one to store acorns for our family to eat."

"There are game sticks in the old basket," says Tara. "Can we put game sticks in my basket, too?"

"Yes," says Grandmother. "The sticks are special. They are part of a game that your ancestors played long ago. One child hides the sticks behind his or her back. The others guess which hand holds the marked sticks. The same game is still played today."

"Now I know why you have these things," says Tara. "They are treasures of our past."

1. What makes something a treasure?
2. What things are treasures to you?

CITIZENSHIP
Making Choices

Cleaning Up

Tara's friends are working together to help her clean out the attic in her home. They are having a problem deciding what to do. They can save an item, throw it out, or give it to a person who might need it. How would you help the friends decide what to do?

Here's Tara's baby book.

There are pieces missing from this puzzle.

Relatives

BY JEFF MOSS

(A Poem To Say Fast When You Want To Show Off)
My father's and mother's sisters and brothers
Are called my uncles and aunts
(Except when they're called *ma tante* and *mon oncle*
Which happens if they're in France.)
Now the daughters and sons of my uncles and aunts
Are my cousins. (Confusion increases—
Since if you're my mother or if you're my Dad,
Then those cousins are nephews and nieces.)

UNIT 1 REVIEW

Thinking About Words

Tell if each sentence is true or false. If the sentence is false, tell how to make it true.

1. Traditions are ways of doing things.

2. A **community** is always small.

3. Ancestors are relatives who lived before you were born.

4. A tree is a form of **transportation**.

5. History is what happened in the past.

6. A **suburb** is outside of a city.

7. A **neighborhood** has homes.

Thinking About Ideas

1. How can traditions be part of a family's history?

2. What can a family tree show?

3. Name two kinds of communities.

4. Name a form of transportation families use today and another families used in the past.

5. Why might some families want to know where their ancestors came from?

6. Why might a family save things?

Think about a real or storybook family. What do you know about the history of the family or its members?

Using Skills

Reviewing Finding Alike and Different

1. How are the pictures alike?

2. How are the pictures different?

Make Your Own!

- Fold a sheet of paper in half.
- Draw a kind of transportation a family might have used long ago on one side of the paper.
- Trade your drawing with a partner.
- Draw a different kind of transportation a family might use today on the other side of your partner's paper.
- Look at the drawings with your partner. Tell how the four kinds of transportation are alike. Tell how they are different.

Using Skills

Reviewing Using Calendars

1. How many days does November have?

2. On what day of the week does November begin?

3. Jack's family is going on a trip. He circled the day. When is the trip?

4. What special day is November 25?

5. On what day of the week will December start?

UNIT REVIEW PROJECT
Make a Fold-Out Picture Book

- Fold two sheets of white paper in half the long way.
- Cut the sheets along the fold to make four pieces.
- Fold the pieces in half the short way.
- Tape the edges of the pieces together to make a long strip.
- Draw important events in your own life on each part.
- Glue on construction paper covers.
- Write your name on the cover.
- Refold the strip to make a book.

Reading on Your Own

You can look for these books at your library.

UNIT TWO

Earth, Our Home

Sacramento

Key Words

capital

river

lake

plain

mountain

hill

valley

peninsula

island

natural resource

Fifty States, One Country

Meet Eddie and Julia. They are neighbors. They live in a city called Sacramento in the state of California. Find Sacramento on the map.

"Sacramento is an important city in California," says Eddie. "This is because Sacramento is the **capital** of our state."

A capital is where the leaders of a state work.

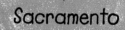

Sacramento

40

In school Julia drew pictures about California. Julia drew the state flag. "It stands for California," she says. "The flag shows a bear and a star."

Like other states, California has a state bird, a state flower, and a state tree. These are California's state symbols. You can see them in Julia's pictures.

"We live in a city and a state," says Eddie.
"We also live in the United States. The United
States is the name of our country. The United
States is made up of 50 different states."

Look at the map. Do you see California? It is
one of the 50 states. Name some other states.

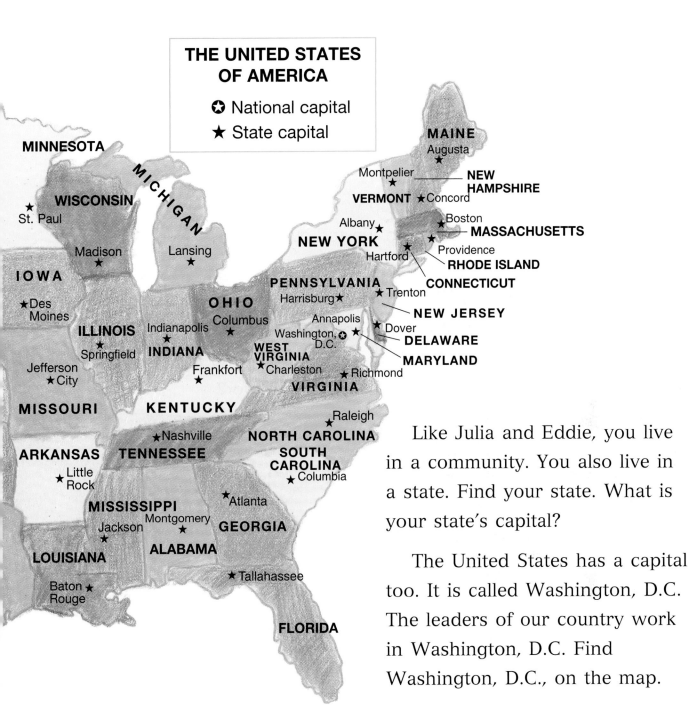

THE UNITED STATES OF AMERICA

✪ National capital
★ State capital

Like Julia and Eddie, you live in a community. You also live in a state. Find your state. What is your state's capital?

The United States has a capital too. It is called Washington, D.C. The leaders of our country work in Washington, D.C. Find Washington, D.C., on the map.

1. What are three names for the place where you live?

2. Find your state on the map. Which states touch your state?

Using a Compass Rose

A **compass rose** shows directions on a map. The compass rose on this map will help Julia. She and her family are planning a trip to Louisiana.

Look at the map below. Do you see the arrows on it? They are part of a compass rose. It helps show where directions are. The **N** on the compass rose stands for north. The **S** stands for south. The **E** stands for east. What does the **W** stand for?

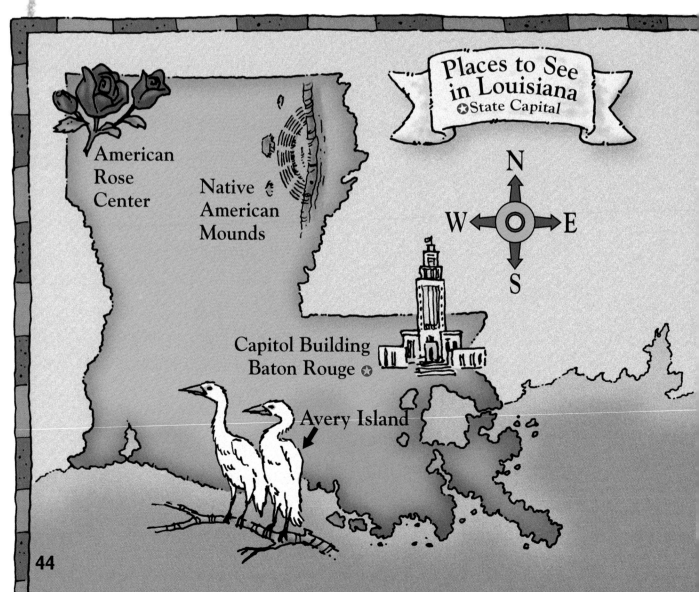

Places to See in Louisiana
⭐State Capital

American Rose Center

Native American Mounds

Capitol Building Baton Rouge ⭐

Avery Island

Julia looks for the capital city of Baton Rouge. Find Baton Rouge on the map. Is it in the east or west part of Louisiana?

Trying the Skill

Use the compass rose to answer the questions.

1. The Native American Mounds are thousands of years old. Are they north or south of Avery Island?

2. Julia's family visits the American Rose Center. Is it east or west of the Native American Mounds?

3. Birds called egrets live on Avery Island. Is that north or south of Baton Rouge?

Magnolia
State Flower

Bald Cypress
State Tree

LOUISIANA

Brown Pelican
State Bird

A World of Countries

In Sacramento, Eddie and Julia often do things together because they are neighbors. Countries have neighbors too. The map shows two neighbors of the United States. To the north is the country of Canada. The other neighbor is Mexico. In what direction is Mexico from the United States?

NORTH AMERICA

ARCTIC OCEAN

GREENLAND

ALASKA (U.S.)

CANADA

N
W   E
S

UNITED STATES

ATLANTIC OCEAN

HAWAII (U.S.)

Gulf of Mexico

WEST INDIES

MEXICO

PACIFIC OCEAN

CENTRAL AMERICA

The people in these three countries have their own special ways of doing things. They have their own special days and enjoy different foods. They play their favorite games too. But like most neighbors, the three countries also share things. Have you ever seen a rodeo? Rodeos in the United States had their beginnings in Mexico. Do you like to play ice hockey? That is a game that was started in Canada.

Which game from our country would you like to share with someone in Canada or Mexico?

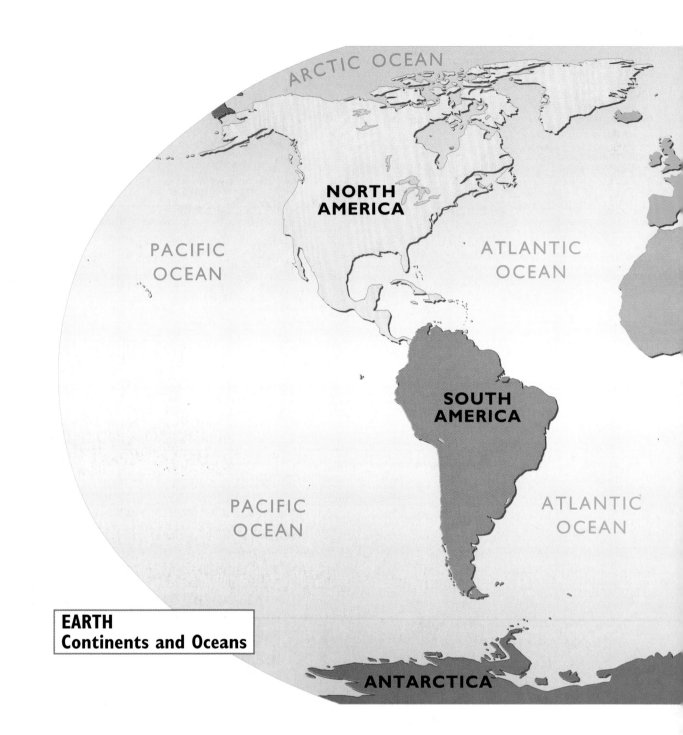

EARTH
Continents and Oceans

The United States and its neighbors are on the continent of North America. North America is just one of Earth's continents. Altogether, there are seven continents on Earth. Use the map to help you name the seven continents.

Most of Earth is covered by water. Find and name the four oceans. Which three oceans are nearest to North America? In what directions are these oceans from North America?

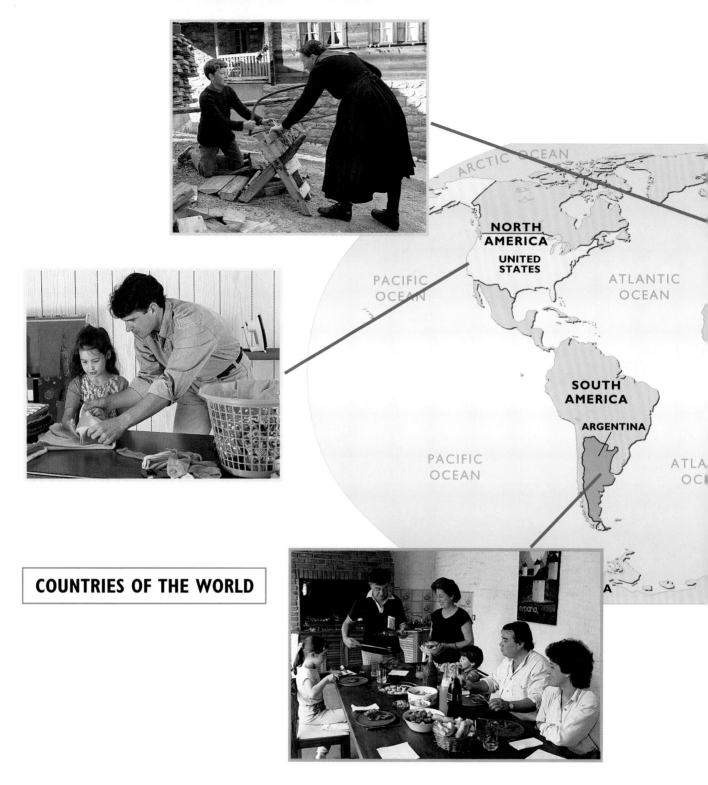

COUNTRIES OF THE WORLD

As you know, Eddie and Julia live in our country. The United States is on the continent of North America.

Look at the countries on the map. They are just a few of the countries in the world. On which continent is each country found?

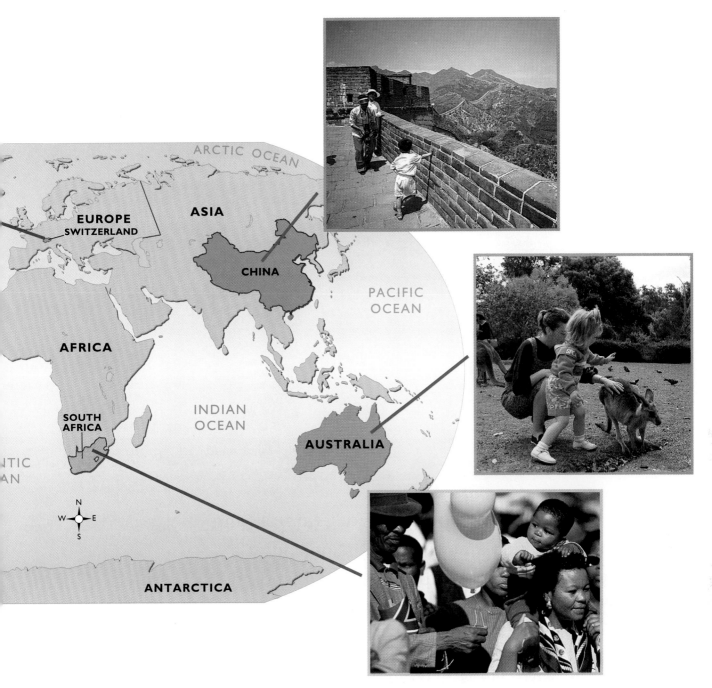

There are many people to meet in each country. Look at the pictures on these pages. How are the families from each country like yours? In what ways might they be different?

1. Name a country on another continent.

2. What country would you like to visit? Why?

Looking at Earth

It is a rainy day. Julia and Eddie are playing indoors at Eddie's house. Julia is looking at a globe. She sees the shapes of Earth's land and water on the globe.

Eddie is taping pictures of Earth's land and water to yarn. He is making a mobile. A mobile is a kind of art work with moving parts.

Julia points to a large body of water on the globe. "That's an ocean," she says. Julia looks at a picture of an ocean on Eddie's mobile.

Ocean

River

Julia points to another body of water on the globe. "This is a **river**," she says.

Eddie shows her a river on his mobile. He says, "A river is a long body of water that flows across the land. Most rivers flow into a larger body of water, like an ocean."

Eddie's mobile also shows a **lake**. A lake is a body of water with land all around it. A lake is smaller than an ocean. All rivers and most lakes have fresh water.

Lake

Plain

Eddie sees that the land on Earth is not all the same. Some of it is flat. This kind of land is called a **plain**. "We live on a plain," Eddie says to Julia.

Some land is higher than a plain. The highest kind of land is a **mountain**.

Mountain

A **hill** is land higher than land around it.
A hill is lower than a mountain.

Hill

"Do you know what a **valley** is?" Eddie asks Julia. He explains that a valley is low land between hills or mountains.

Valley

55

Peninsula

"Look at this land that is sticking out," says Julia. "It's called a **peninsula**."

A peninsula is land that has water on three sides. One side of a peninsula is joined to a larger body of land.

Island

"I know what this is," Julia tells Eddie. "It's an **island**. An island is land that has water all around it."

Eddie finishes his mobile. It is time for Julia to go home. She puts on her raincoat. Julia is dressing for the weather. Today the weather is rainy. Weather may also be sunny, cloudy, or snowy. The weather is also how hot or cold it is outside. What kind of weather do you like best?

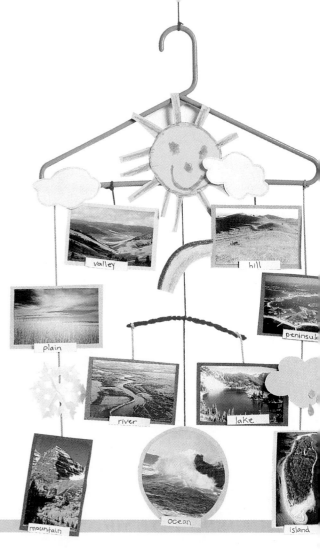

?

1. Which kind of land has water all around it? Which kind of water has land all around it?

2. What kind of water and land are near your community?

GEOGRAPHY SKILLS
Using Landform Maps

The different kinds of land on Earth are called landforms. Julia found some of Earth's landforms on a globe. Another way to find landforms is to use a landform map.

Most landform maps use color symbols to show different kinds of land.

Green shows plains.

Orange shows mountains.

Gold shows hills.

Below is a landform map of the state of Oregon. Find the map key. The color green stands for plains. What does orange stand for?

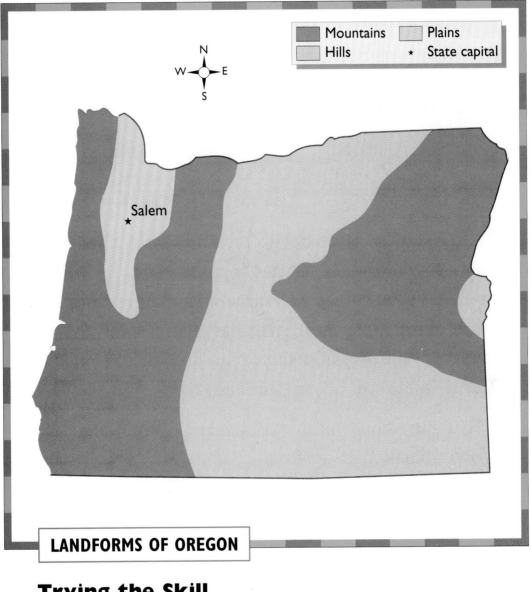

Mountains   **Plains**
Hills   ★ **State capital**

Salem ★

LANDFORMS OF OREGON

Trying the Skill

Use the landform map to answer the questions.

1. What kinds of landforms does Oregon have?

2. On what kind of landform is Salem?

3. Are there more plains or hills in Oregon?

Our Natural Resources

A new house is going up on Eddie and Julia's street. Building a house uses many **natural resources**. A natural resource is something in nature that people use. Earth has many natural resources. Soil, rocks, water, sun, and air are all natural resources. So are animals, trees, and plants.

"The new house is made of wood," says Julia. "Wood comes from trees."

"Our blocks are made of wood too," says Eddie.

"Some houses are made of stone," says Eddie. "Stones are natural resources too."

Bricks are made from clay in the soil. So brick houses are also made from natural resources.

"I know another natural resource," says Julia. "An igloo is made from snow!"

Building houses is just one way that people use natural resources. What ways do you use natural resources?

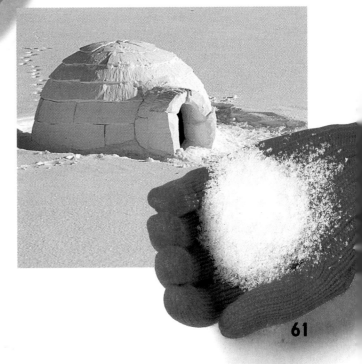

Natural resources are very important. People must use them carefully. We must be careful not to use up our natural resources.

It takes many trees to build a house of wood. Trees grow slowly. You can tell how many years it took a tree to grow. Just count the circles in a tree trunk. Sometimes people plant new trees when they cut trees down. This is one way to save our natural resources.

EDDIE'S TIPS

☑ 1. Pick up litter.

☑ 2. Keep our water clean.

☑ 3. Recycle cans and bottles.

☑ 4. Reuse paper.

☑ 5. Plant a tree.

Eddie has started a list of other ways to care for natural resources. Do you do the things on the list? What ideas could you add to this list?

1. Name two natural resources that you have used.

2. Why is it important to care for natural resources?

Making a Difference

Nashville

TENNESSEE

Melissa and the Kid's Yard

Melissa Poe lives in the city of Nashville, in the state of Tennessee. When Melissa was nine years old, she began working for a cleaner world. Melissa leads a group called Kids F.A.C.E. The name stands for Kids For A Clean Environment. The group has members all over the country.

One day Melissa was playing outside. She thought it would be nice to have a place where animals could find water, food, and shelter. She also wanted a place where children could watch animals. She called this place Kid's Yard.

Some people in Nashville gave the group a big field for the first Kid's Yard. There they planted trees, bushes, and flowers. "As the plants grow," Melissa said, "their berries and leaves will bring birds, butterflies, and bugs. Animals will come, and birds will build nests for their babies."

Melissa is spreading her ideas. A business helped her print many posters for the group. The posters tell how to start a Kid's Yard. Melissa sends them to schools and groups. She also sends them to anyone who writes to her. "Trees, animals, and people all need each other," she said. "We can all help planet Earth."

This Is My House

Written and illustrated by
Arthur Dorros

from

THIS IS MY HOUSE

Written and illustrated by Arthur Dorros

This is my house. My grandfather built it. When we put on a new roof, the house will keep us warm and dry again.

A house on wheels in Yugoslavia

A thatch house in Fiji

A tree house in the Solomon Islands

People make houses out of whatever they can find. There are houses with walls of stone, or wood, or mud, or grass.

There are houses with walls of paper, walls of snow, even houses on wheels.

Mud houses in Cameroon

Stone houses in Israel

An igloo in Canada

Brick houses in China

Greetings from Seattle

A tent in Tibet

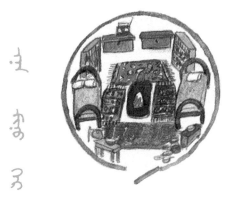

*What's in
a yurt*

AY-neh MIH-nee GER

This is my house.

Our tent in the mountains has a door. A
floor and carpets keep us off the cold ground.
We can carry our tent, called a *yurt,*
when we move.

MONGOLIA

Esta casa é minha.
EHS-tah CAH-zah EH MEEN-yah.
This is my house.

My whole house is made of plants. Where we live, there are plants all around us. We use dried plants called *thatch* to cover the roof.

Many families live together in our house.

BRAZIL

70

Dette er mitt hus.
DETT-teh AIR MITT HOOS
This is my house.

Our wooden house has a roof that grows. It is covered with moss and other plants.

NORWAY

EGYPT

هـذا منزلي .
HAH-zah mon-ZILL-ee
This is my house.

We need to add new thatch to the roof of our stone house every year. The thatch wears away, but the stone doesn't. A stone building can last for thousands of years.

Esta es mi casa.
EHS-tah EHS MEE CAH-sah
This is my house.

Our house is made of mud. It is almost finished. We form *adobe* bricks from wet mud. Then the bricks are dried in the sunlight. We fill cracks and smooth the walls with more mud.

After our day's work, we visit my grandmother. She built her adobe house by herself.

MEXICO

呢間係我間屋

NEE GAN HIGH EENN'AW GAN AWK
This is my house.

The building I live in is made of cement and steel. Families live in groups of rooms called *apartments* on each floor.

Workers on bamboo scaffolding thirty floors high are finishing another apartment building. People from apartments below hang laundry on the scaffolding.

HONG KONG

74

A house can be big or small, in the country or in a city. Wherever it is, the people who live in a house make it their home.

UNIT 2 REVIEW

Thinking About Words

Tell if each sentence is true or false. If the sentence is false, tell how to make it true.

1. Each state has a **capital**.

2. A **lake** is bigger than an ocean.

3. A **mountain** is higher than a **hill**.

4. A **peninsula** has water on only one side.

5. An **island** is surrounded by water.

6. A **valley** is low land between two **plains**.

7. Animals, plants, and trees are **natural resources**.

8. A **river** is a long body of fresh water.

Thinking About Ideas

1. How many states does our country have?

2. What is the capital of the United States?

3. In what direction is Canada from the United States?

4. What are two ways that people use natural resources?

5. What are two ways to care for natural resources?

Tell some ways that you could help to save natural resources at home and at school.

Using Skills

Reviewing Using a Compass Rose

1. Is the Great Salt Lake in the north or south part of the state?

2. Find the dinosaur on the map. Is this place in the east or the west part of Utah?

3. Is Dixie National Forest north or south of the Great Salt Lake?

4. Which place is in the most south part of Utah?

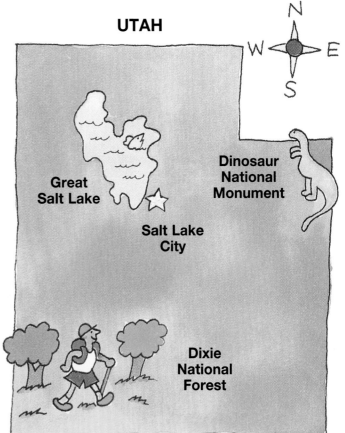

UTAH

Great Salt Lake

Dinosaur National Monument

Salt Lake City

Dixie National Forest

Make Your Own!

- Draw the shape of your classroom.
- Draw the desks, windows, and door.
- Make a compass rose.

Using Skills

Reviewing Using Landform Maps

1. What does gold stand for on the map?

2. What kinds of landforms does California have?

3. What kind of land is in the west part of California?

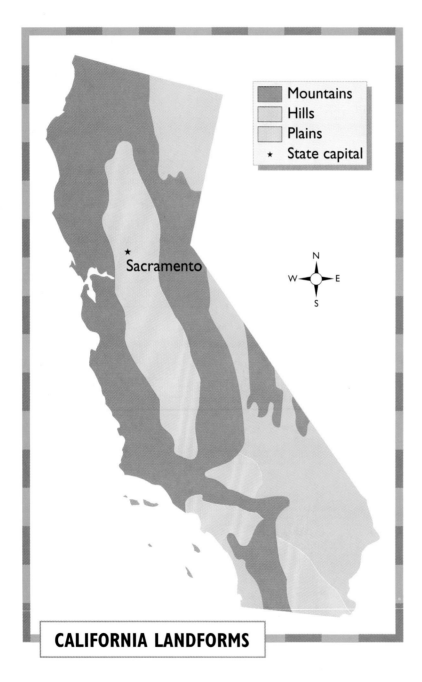

CALIFORNIA LANDFORMS

UNIT REVIEW PROJECT

Make Up a New Continent

- On a large piece of paper, draw the outline of your new continent.
- On different paper, draw landforms for your continent.
- Color the landforms and cut them out.
- Glue the landforms onto your continent.
- Write the name of your continent on the page.
- Ask a partner to name the landforms on your continent.

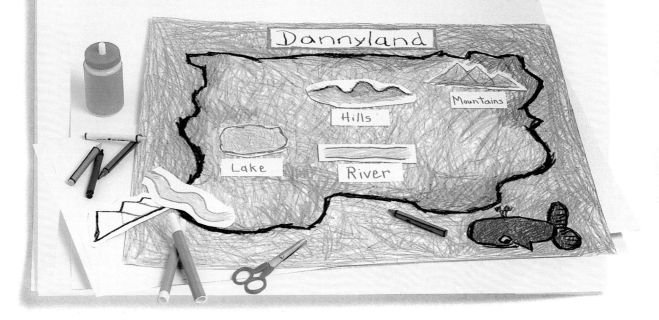

Reading on Your Own

You can look for these books at your library.

A Working World

Key Words

goods

service

factory

trade

needs

shelter

wants

MEXICO

Let's go!

A Trip to the Market

Ann and her parents live in the city of San Francisco. This city is in the state of California. They are shopping at an outdoor market.

This market is a busy place. Many people come here to sell things. Others come here to buy things. Ann looks at the different goods that are for sale. Goods are things that people make or grow.

Ann helps her parents to pick out some corn. They will have corn with dinner tonight.

Ann stops by the bread stand. "May I pick out some bread?" Ann asks her mother. "It smells so good!"

At the next stand Ann's father sees some strawberry jam. "This is my favorite kind," he says. "We can put it on the bread."

That looks good!

83

Thank you!

You're welcome.

Ann's father buys the jam. "People who sell things are performing a **service**," says Ann's father.

"What's a service?" Ann asks.

"A service is something useful that people do for others," her father says. "People can earn money when they make things to sell or do services for others."

Barbers and doctors do services for others.

"There are many community service workers," says Ann's mother. "Do you see any here?"

Ann looks around the market. "I see a community service worker," she says. "A police officer is giving a woman directions!" Ann wonders what the woman is looking for at the market.

Teachers and firefighters are community service workers.

Over there.

Thank you.

1. What is a service?

2. Tell about a market in your community. How is it like the market that Ann went to? How is it different?

STUDY SKILLS
Using Flow Charts

At the market Ann and her parents bought milk. One way to show what happens to milk before it gets to the market is on a **flow chart**. A flow chart shows the order in which things flow, or happen.

From Cow to Carton

1. The farmer uses a machine to milk the cow.

2. A truck driver takes the milk to the dairy plant.

3. At the plant, people use machines to put the milk into bottles or cartons.

The flow chart above shows how milk travels from the farm to the dairy plant. To read the flow chart, start at number 1. In step 1 the farmer uses a machine to milk the cow. What is the next step?

Trying the Skill

What happens to milk after it is put into bottles or cartons at the dairy? Use the flow chart on this page to answer the questions.

From Market to Home

1. A truck driver takes the milk to the market.

2. People buy the milk.

3. People take the milk home to drink.

1. What happens after the truck driver takes the milk to the market?

2. What is the last step in the flow chart?

3. How did the flow chart help you to find the answer to the last two questions?

From the Farm

Today Ann's parents bought some corn at the market. Before food gets to the market, someone has to grow or make the food.

The farmer plows the soil.

GROWING CORN

The farmer plants the seeds.

Ann is looking for pictures of people growing corn. She decides to make a flow chart. The chart shows some of the steps of growing corn.

Look at step 4. The farmer's job is almost done. What do you think happens next?

The farmer waters the corn.

The farmer picks the corn.

After the farmer picks the corn, the corn is ready to sell. The farmer loads it onto a big truck to take to the market. Trucks are just one kind of transportation farmers use. Planes, trains, and ships are also ways to move goods from place to place.

The farmer drives the corn to the market.

Tonight Ann and her parents eat corn with dinner. "Mmmm!" It tastes good!

1. How does food get from a farm to a market?

2. Draw a flow chart showing how food gets from the store to your house.

GEOGRAPHY SKILLS
Following Routes on a Map

Carl is a truck driver. Sometimes, Carl brings corn from a farm to a store. Carl gets to the store by following a **route**. A route is a way of going from one place to another. This map shows Carl's route.

Find Carl's truck. He starts on Walnut Drive. Then he turns right on Acorn Lane. Where does he go next?

Truck Route

CARL'S TRUCKING

HILLTOP FARM

WALNUT DRIVE

JACKSON POND

ACORN LANE

CHURCH

HAYTOWN ROAD

JACKSON HIGHWAY

BRANDON APARTMENTS

N
W E
S

BRANDON STREET

Trying the Skill

Use the map to answer the questions.

1. What building does Carl pass on the corner of Hillside Avenue and Brandon Street?

2. Find another route Carl could take to the store.

3. How does following a route on a map help Carl? How might it help you?

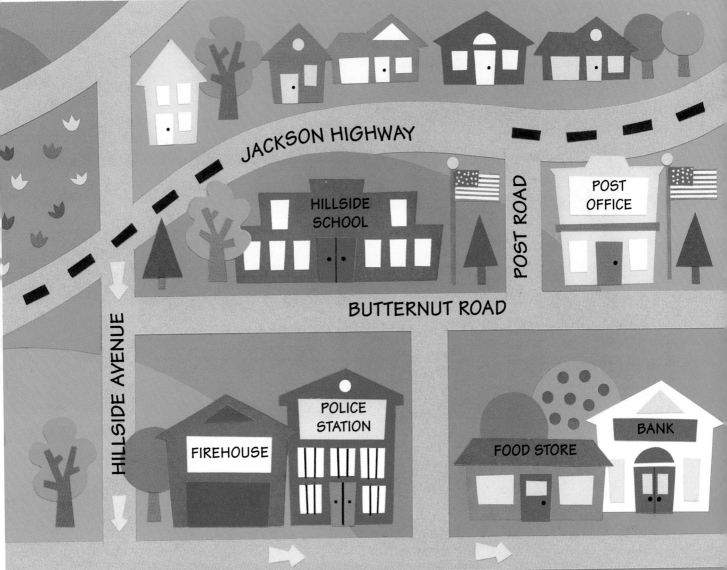

From the Factory

Sometimes farmers bring their corn to a store.
Other times they bring it to a **factory**. A factory
is a building where things are made. The workers in
a factory put corn into cans.

Ann wonders what happens to corn in a factory.
Ann's mother tells her how to learn about corn on the
computer. The computer has a guide called Ginny.
Ginny shows Ann a factory that puts corn into cans.

94

My name is Ginny. Welcome to the factory. Here are some of the steps in making canned corn. First, workers make sure the corn cobs go smoothly into machines that will cut the corn.

Next the corn is cut. Workers sort the cut corn to make sure each piece is good. Everyone works together carefully to get the corn ready to be put into cans.

A machine fills cans with corn. Other machines seal the cans. Then, the cans are heated to keep the corn from spoiling. Finally, the cans are cooled. At last, drivers bring the cans to the store in trucks.

Ann is glad that she visited a factory by computer! She didn't need any transportation to get to the factory!

?

1. What happens at a factory?

2. Why is it important for factory workers to work well together?

CITIZENSHIP
Making a Difference

La Conner

WASHINGTON

GIRAFFES HELP OTHERS

The Giraffe Club meets every Tuesday afternoon at La Conner Elementary School. La Conner is a city in the state of Washington. Members begin their meeting by saying these words.

"I promise to stick my neck out to make a difference. I will help people, animals, and my environment to make the world a better place to live."

The Giraffes work together to help people. Many of the people who they help live at Friendship House. This is a place where families without homes, food, and money can live. Club members collect canned food. Then they give the food to the families. They also buy the families turkeys for Thanksgiving dinner.

Giraffes at school library

Once a year, the Giraffes get very dirty digging in the fields. A farmer lets them come to his farm to pick potatoes. The club can have any potatoes that farm machines leave unpicked in the fields. Giraffes fill two big trucks with potatoes. They give them to Friendship House and Swinomish Indian Senior Center.

On their birthdays children at Friendship House get party trimmings and presents from the Giraffes. The club also gives presents to families at Friendship House in December.

One Giraffe member, Matika Wilbur, thinks everyone should help others. She says, "It will make you feel good about yourself."

Matika at Senior Center

Trading Goods

Ann and her mother are making popcorn. "We grow lots of corn in the United States," says Ann's mother. "But there are some foods that do not grow in our country. You know one. Do you remember what you gave to me for my birthday?"

"Brazil nuts!" says Ann.

"Yes! My favorite nut!" says Ann's mother. Ann's mother gets her jar of Brazil nuts from the shelf. "One place where these nuts grow is in Brazil. Brazil is a country in South America."

"How do countries get things they cannot grow or make?" asks Ann.

"They **trade**," says Ann's mother. "Trade is sending goods to a country and then getting other goods back. Countries need to trade with each other to get goods they do not have. Our country trades with Brazil. Brazil sells nuts and other goods to the United States. The United States sells corn and other goods to Brazil."

"I'll trade you a piece of popcorn for a Brazil nut!" says Ann.

Ann's mother shows her a map of Brazil.

"How do the nuts get here from Brazil?" asks Ann. "Brazil is far away."

"Some foods and goods are sent by ship or plane," explains her mother. "Goods are also sent over the land by trains or trucks."

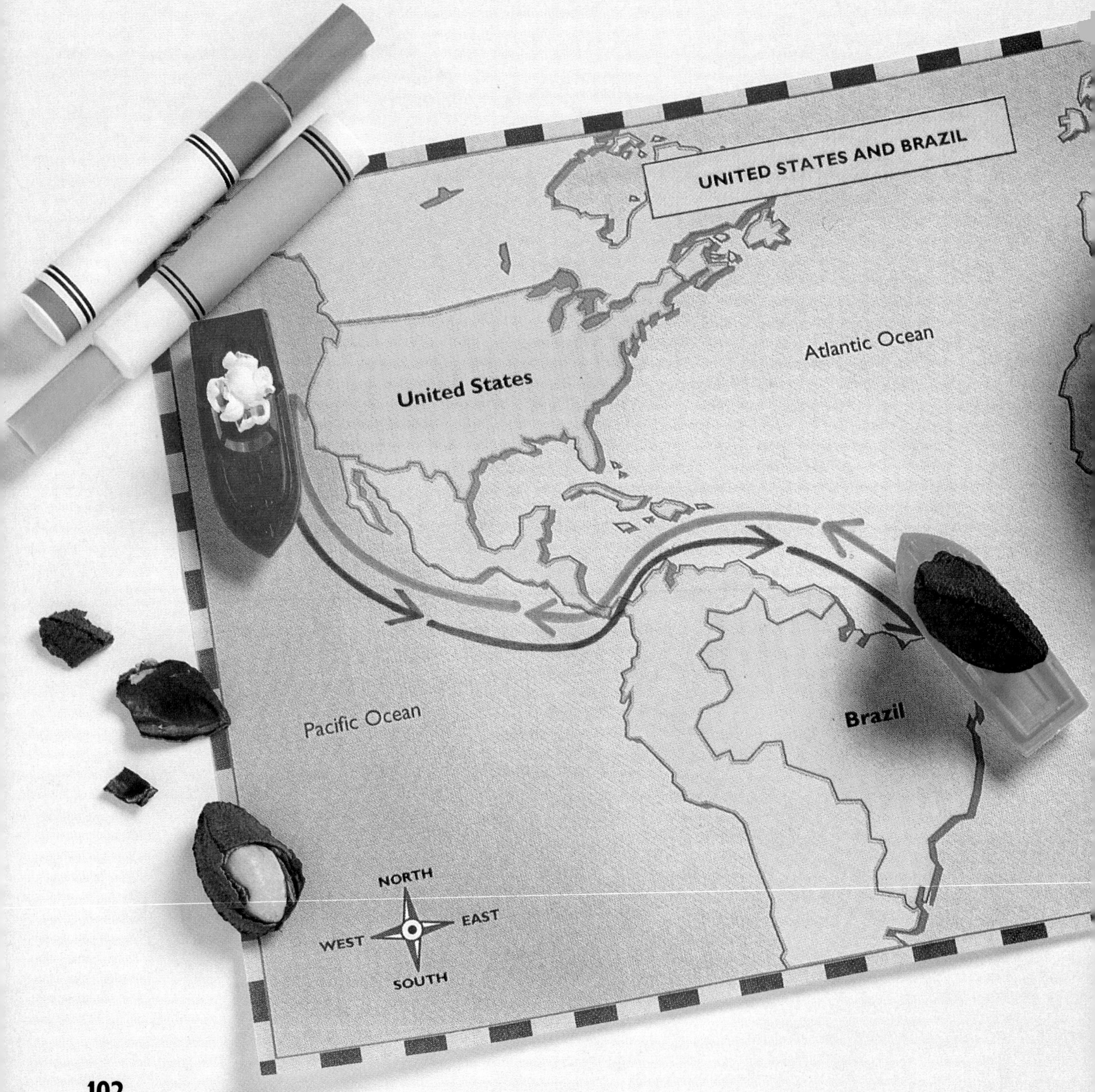

UNITED STATES AND BRAZIL

United States

Atlantic Ocean

Pacific Ocean

Brazil

NORTH

WEST — EAST

SOUTH

Ann traces the route from Brazil to her community in the United States on the map. She and her mother eat popcorn and Brazil nuts. They are glad that countries trade so that they can enjoy goods from other places.

1. What types of transportation are used to trade goods?

2. Why do countries trade? What might happen if countries did not trade?

Work, Money, and You

Ouch! Ann's shoes are tight. "You're growing so fast," says her father. "You need new shoes."

All people have **needs**. A need is something you must have to live. Clothing is one kind of need. Food is another. Everyone needs food to stay healthy and to grow. People need a place to live too. This is called **shelter**. Ann and her family live in an apartment house.

People also have other needs. Two important ones are love and care.

Ann and her parents drive to the mall. They buy Ann new shoes there. At the mall Ann sees some flowers. "Let's buy them for Grandma," she says. "She will like them."

Besides needs, people also have **wants**. Wants are things people would like to have but do not need to live. Flowers and toys are wants. Name some other wants.

How do people pay for things they need and want? Most people work at jobs. They earn money from working. They use this money to pay for needs such as food, shelter, and clothing. They earn money to pay for wants like flowers and toys too.

Ann's father fixes computers to earn money. Her mother works in a clothing store two days a week. Name some other jobs that people do.

Ann's birthday is coming. Her parents are saving money to buy her a new bicycle. They put some money in the bank each month. Then they will have enough money to buy the bicycle for Ann's birthday. What a nice surprise that will be!

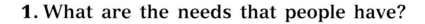

1. What are the needs that people have?

2. How do some people earn money?

THINKING SKILLS
Sorting Things into Groups

Ann has pictures of people. She sorted the pictures into groups. When you sort things, you put them into groups of things that are alike.

To sort, Ann first looked at one picture. She saw that the picture showed a worker making goods. Then she looked at the other pictures. Ann found another picture of a worker growing goods. These pictures are a group. Ann named the group "Workers Making or Growing Goods." She found one more picture that went in this group.

Look at the other pictures. In what way are they alike? What might you name this group of pictures?

Trying the Skill

Ann has pictures of people who make money doing different jobs. Help her sort the pictures on this page into two groups.

1. How are the pictures in each group alike?

2. Name each group.

3. How did you sort these things into groups?

MY MAMI TAKES ME TO THE BAKERY

by Charlotte Pomerantz
picture by Byron Barton

Let's buy pan de agua, daughter.
Pan is bread and agua, water.
Good fresh bread of flour and water.
Good fresh pan de agua, daughter.

Inside the panadería,
There's the hot sweet smell of pan.
Good day, says the plump panadero.
(The baker's a very nice man.)

How many loaves, Señora, he asks:
Uno . . . dos?
Dos? Sí, sí.
Two, por favor, says my mami.
Two loaves for my daughter and me.

UNIT 3 REVIEW

Thinking About Words

Choose one word to go with each clue below.

goods	**service**	**factory**	**shelter**
trade	**wants**	**needs**	

1. A building where things are made
2. A place to live
3. Things that people make and grow
4. Sending goods to a country and getting other goods back
5. Something useful that people do for others
6. Things you would like to have but do not need to live
7. Things you must have to live

Thinking About Ideas

1. How are goods different from services?
2. Name three kinds of transportation that move goods.
3. How are wants different from needs?
4. How do we get goods from other countries?

Think about a service you could do in your neighborhood. Tell how you would do it.

Using Skills

Reviewing Following Routes on a Map

This map shows a route Jan takes from her apartment building to go to the clothing store.

1. What can Jan get at the corner of Hope Street and Glen Road?
2. Where does she go after Hope Street?
3. What other route can Jan take to the store?

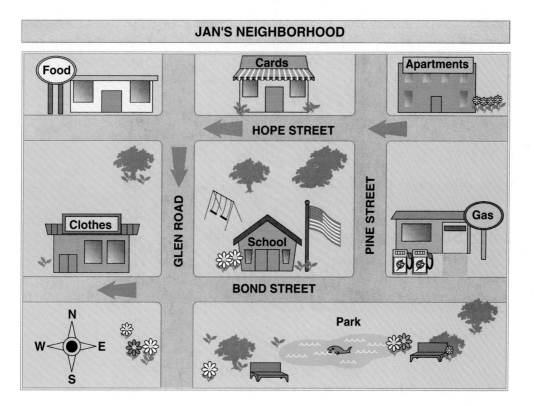

JAN'S NEIGHBORHOOD

Food · Cards · Apartments

HOPE STREET

GLEN ROAD · PINE STREET

Clothes · School · Gas

BOND STREET

N W E S · Park

Make Your Own!

- Draw a map of a make-believe house.
- Draw a route to show how to get from the front door to the kitchen.

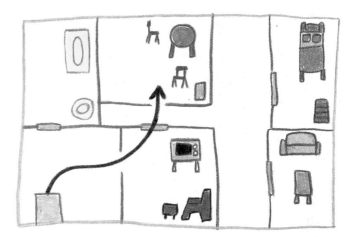

Using Skills

Reviewing Using Flow Charts

Buying Shoes

1. The shopper looks at the shoes.

2. The shopper tries on the shoes.

3. The shopper buys the shoes.

1. What does the shopper do first?

2. What does she do after she looks at the shoes?

3. Does the shopper pay for the shoes before or after she tries them on?

Reviewing Sorting Things into Groups

1. Sort the things below into two groups.

2. How are the pictures in each group alike?

3. Name each group.

Unit Review Project

Selling Goods or Services

- Draw the inside of a store on a piece of paper. Include places where you can show goods or services.
- Glue your store to the inside of a shoebox.
- Make a sign for your store. Glue it onto the shoebox.
- Draw or find pictures of your store's goods or services.
- Make or find goods for your store.
- Glue the pictures and goods onto your store.

Reading on Your Own

You can look for these books at your library.

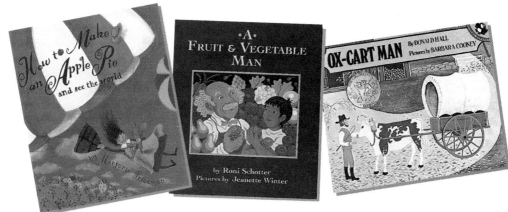

UNIT FOUR

We the People

$2.00
+ TAX

Key Words

citizen

law

vote

tax

government

President

monument

museum

White House

Congress

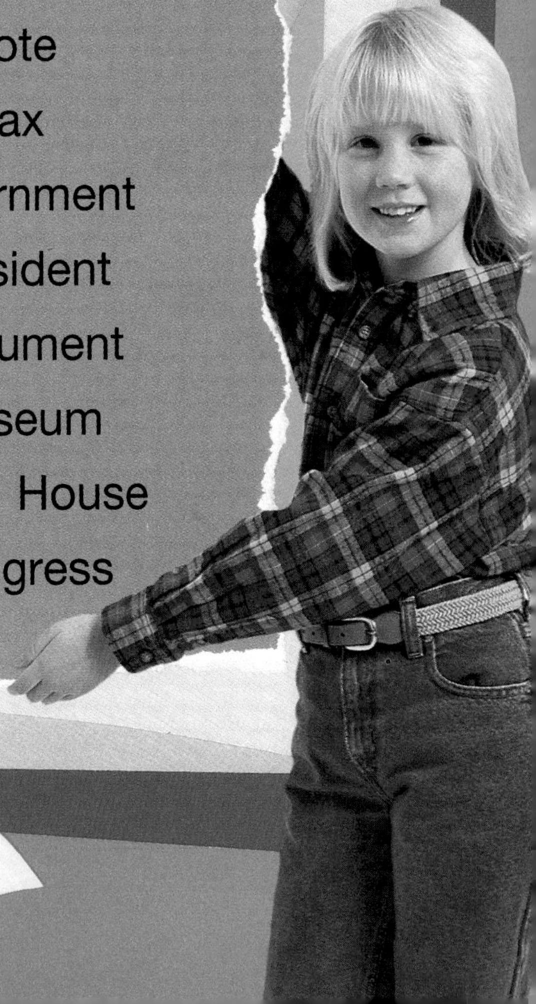

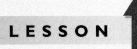

Solving a City Problem

Jake lives in Charlotte, North Carolina.
Charlotte is the largest city in North Carolina.
The citizens of Charlotte work together to solve
problems in their city. Citizens are people who are
members of a
community, state,
or country.

Jake is making a scrapbook
of citizens who solve problems
in Charlotte. Two citizens in
Jake's scrapbook are students.
Their names are Lila and
Nadia Hauck. Lila and
Nadia are twin sisters.

Lila and Nadia thought that the corner where their school bus stopped was not safe. Cars went by without stopping. They talked about the problem with their father. The girls and their father believed that a stop sign would make the corner safer. It is a **law** for cars to stop at a stop sign. Laws are rules for a community, state, or country.

Lila, Nadia, and their father decided to work together. They needed to get the leaders of the city to agree that a stop sign was needed. A leader is a person who is in charge of things.

Lila and Nadia

119

First Lila, Nadia, and their father talked to their neighbors. They explained the problem. They asked citizens to sign a petition to give to the city's leaders. A petition is a special letter that many people sign. The petition said that people wanted a stop sign at the corner.

Next Lila and her father went to the city council. A city council is a group of citizens who run the city. They are the city leaders. The city council meets to talk about city problems. The members make laws to help solve the problems. The people of the city must then follow the laws.

Lila spoke at a city council meeting. She explained the problem in her neighborhood. She asked the city council for a stop sign. "Please put up the sign," she said, "so no one will get hurt."

Lila and her dad

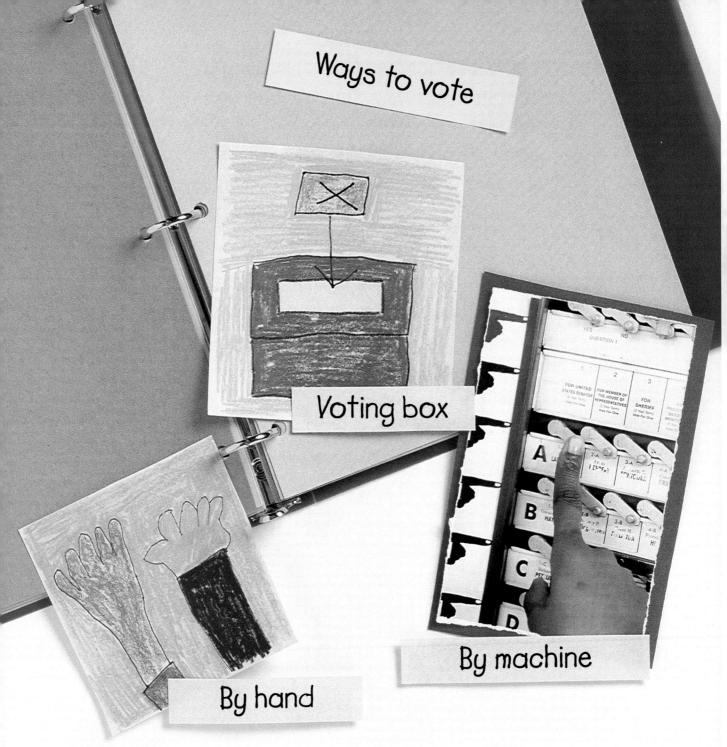

Ways to vote

Voting box

By hand

By machine

The members of the city council listened to Lila. They listened to her father too. They read the petition people had signed. Then they talked about the problem. The city council decided to **vote** on the new stop sign. To vote is to choose something. The city council would vote whether or not to put up a stop sign.

The city council voted to put up the stop sign. They used **tax** money to pay for the sign. A tax is money that people pay to the community. The community leaders use tax money to pay service workers, like the people who put up the stop sign. They also use the money to pay for things that the community needs.

Today, Charlotte, North Carolina, has a new stop sign. Thanks to Lila and Nadia, it is safer to cross the street in their neighborhood. Jake is glad that Lila and Nadia helped to solve a problem in their community. What problems can you help solve in your community?

The stop sign!

1. **What is a leader?**

2. **What can you or other people do to solve problems in your community?**

THINKING SKILLS
Putting Things in Order

Jake drew pictures of how Lila and Nadia helped to get a stop sign put up in Charlotte. Jake wanted to put the pictures in order. You can put things in order by size, time, or other ways.

Jake looked at each picture. He wanted to put them in order by time. Jake looked for the thing that happened first. First Lila and Nadia asked people to sign a petition to the city council. Next Jake looked for the thing that happened next. This is the picture of the city council voting. What happened last?

Trying the Skill

Jake drew some pictures of cars and a bus stopping at the new stop sign. Jake needs to put the pictures in order. Help him to do it.

1. Do you want to order the pictures by size or time?

2. Which picture comes first?

3. How did you put these pictures in order? Why?

Our Country's Government

Jake is visiting his grandfather. Jake shows his scrapbook to his grandfather. "I have a scrapbook too," says his grandfather. "Scrapbooks are fun."

Jake points to the newspaper story about Lila. "Lila worked with the city council to change things," Jake says.

"The city council is part of the **government** in Charlotte," says his grandfather. "A government is the group of people in charge of running a community, state, or country. Citizens vote for our government leaders. You can vote when you are 18 years old."

"Long ago our country's leaders worked together to make a plan for our government," Jake's grandfather tells him. "This plan is called the United States Constitution. Here is a copy of it in my scrapbook. The Constitution has the country's most important laws. It begins with the words *We the People of the United States*."

"The Constitution also lists the most important rights of our country's citizens. One right is the freedom to worship God as we wish. Voting is another right."

"Here is a picture of your great-grandmother Elsie," says Jake's grandfather. "At first our country's government did not include all people. Women were not allowed to vote when Great-Grandmother Elsie was a young woman. This was a law. Many people thought that this law was not fair. Susan B. Anthony was one of the people who worked to change the law."

Susan B. Anthony

"There were also laws that made it hard for African Americans to vote. People like Martin Luther King, Jr., and Rosa Parks worked for the rights of African Americans. They worked to change the laws. They worked so that all people would have the same rights."

"Many Americans worked together. They helped to change our government to include all people. Now the words *We the People* mean all citizens!"

1. Name three people who helped to change our country's laws.

2. Why did our country's government change? How did these changes help to make our country's government more fair?

STUDY SKILLS
Using Time Lines

Jake's class at school is learning about Susan B. Anthony. They studied something new about her each day for a week. The time line below shows what Jake's class did that week. A time line shows the order in which things happen. The thing that happened first is always on the left of the time line. The thing that happened last is always on the right of the time line.

On Wednesday Jake's class heard a speech by Susan B. Anthony. Find out what Jake's class did on Monday. Look at that day on the time line. Read what it says.

Jake's Week

Sunday	Monday	Tuesday	Wednesday	Thursday	Friday	Saturday
Read a book about Susan B. Anthony	Talked about the book in class	Learned Susan B. Anthony was born February 15, 1820	Heard a speech by Susan B. Anthony	Looked at a copy of a petition	Found out voting law was changed in 1920	Saw TV show on Susan B. Anthony

Trying the Skill

There are four seasons each year. They are fall, winter, spring, and summer. Jake's class studied different people each season. They studied people who helped to change laws in our country. The class studied Susan B. Anthony in the fall. Use the time line below to answer the questions.

People Studied by Jake's Class

Fall	Winter	Spring	Summer
Susan B. Anthony	Martin Luther King, Jr.	Rosa Parks	Abraham Lincoln

1. What person did Jake's class study in the spring?

2. During which season did Jake's class study Martin Luther King, Jr.?

3. Suppose you wanted to write about something you did. How could a time line help you?

Visiting Our Country's Capital

Jake and his family are going on a family vacation to Washington, D.C. This city is the capital of the United States. Our country's government is in Washington, D.C.

"Our country's capital is named after George Washington," says Jake's mother. "He was our first **President**. The President is the most important leader of our country."

Packing for our trip

Washington, D.C., is here!

I live in Charlotte, North Carolina.

The Washington Monument

George Washington

Washington, D.C.

Washington, D.C., has many sights to see. Jake and his family visit many **monuments**. A monument is a building or statue that honors a person or something that happened.

One of Jake's favorite places is the Washington Monument. Who do you think this monument honors? Jake went to the top of this monument. There, he could see across the whole city.

Our country's capital also has a monument to President Abraham Lincoln. Why do you think Abraham Lincoln is honored with a monument?

Jake and his family visit the Vietnam Veterans Memorial. This monument honors people who fought for our country during the Vietnam War. Vietnam is a country in Asia. This monument has the names of all the Americans who died in that war.

Vietnam Veterans Memorial

Abraham Lincoln

Washington, D.C., also has many **museums**. A museum is a building where people go to look at interesting things. There are many museums in Washington, D.C. Some tell about our country's past. Jake and his family visited the National Museum of American History. They also saw many interesting things at the National Air and Space Museum.

National Museum of American History

National Air and Space Museum

Jake could not wait to visit the **White House**. "That's where the President lives and works," he says. "Maybe we will see the President! When I am 18, I will vote to help choose our President."

White House

President Clinton

Jake's family also visits the Capitol Building. "That's where **Congress** meets," Jake's father tells him. "Congress is part of our country's government. The members of Congress make our country's laws. The people of each state vote to choose the members of Congress."

Jake has learned many things on his trip to Washington, D.C. On the way home, Jake dreams about all the wonderful places he has visited.

?

1. Why is Washington, D.C., important?

2. List in order the places that Jake and his family visited.

Capitol Building

Congress

Going home!

Our Country's Flag

Jake saw many American flags in Washington, D.C. "The flag is a symbol for our country," he says.

"That's right," says his mother. "Our flag also has symbols on it. The 50 stars are symbols for our country's 50 states. The 13 stripes are symbols too. They stand for the first 13 states of our country."

"We have an American flag in my classroom," says Jake. "We start the day by saying the *Pledge of Allegiance*. It shows that we honor the flag and our country."

Jake puts his right hand over his heart. "This is how we do it," he says.

I pledge allegiance
to the flag of the
United States of America
and to the Republic
for which it stands,
one Nation under God,
indivisible, with liberty
and justice for all.

1. What does the American flag stand for?

2. Name places where you see American flags. Why do you think people fly the American flag?

Flags of Many Countries

Jake collects flags. Every country has a flag. Each flag is a symbol for that country. Flags often show something important about a country.

This is Canada's flag. The maple leaf in the middle is a symbol of Canada. Many maple trees grow in Canada.

Canada

This is Mexico's flag. The picture in the middle of the flag is a symbol from Mexico's past. This symbol is still important today.

Mexico

Here are some flags from other countries.
What things do you see on each flag?
You can find out what the things
on each flag stand for at
your library.

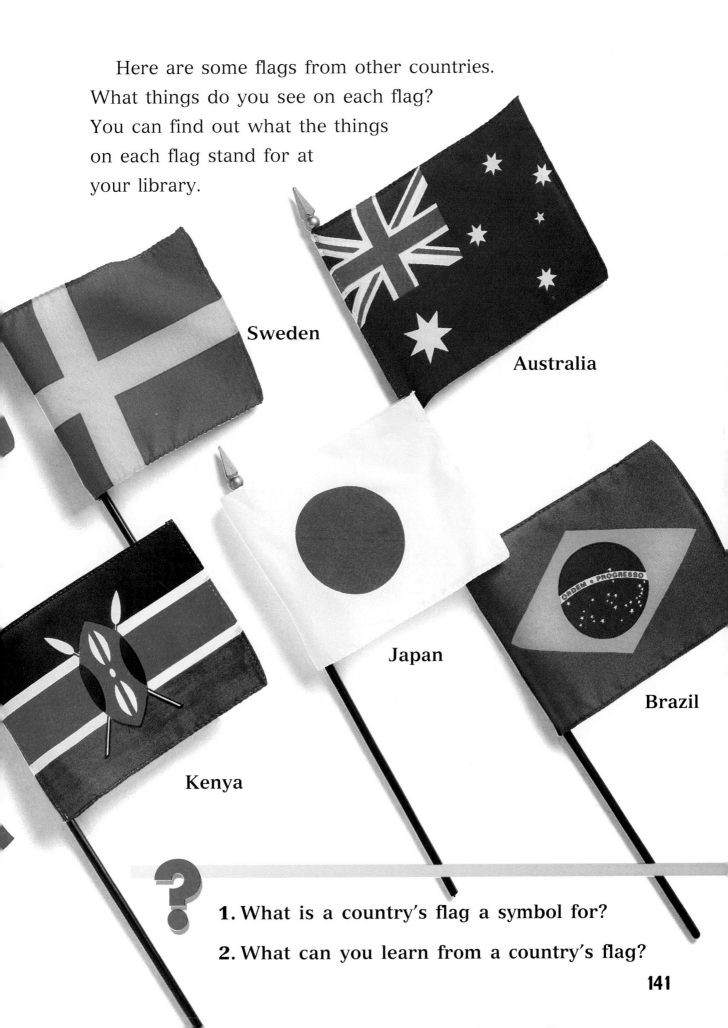

Sweden

Australia

Japan

Brazil

Kenya

1. What is a country's flag a symbol for?

2. What can you learn from a country's flag?

CITIZENSHIP
Making Choices

A Class Flag

Jake's class is making a class flag. They cannot agree on what kind of flag to make. Help Jake's class decide what their flag should look like.

Let's make the flag red. It's a bright color.

Let's show our school colors, green and yellow.

Let's show children that will stand for us.

Our class has a pet fish. Let's put a fish on the flag.

Let's make the flag in the shape of a square.

I think a circle would be nice.

Room 10

The flag can say "Room 10."

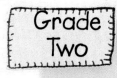

Grade Two

It could also say "Grade Two."

143

CLOSE
With A
Song

The Stars and Stripes Forever

Music by John Philip Sousa
Words by Teresa Jennings

Let's cheer for the red, white and blue! _____

_ May our ban-ner be wav-ing for-ev -

er! Re-mind-ing us how free-dom grew _____

_ from the strug-gles once we knew. _____

Now all should re-mem-ber the

day _____ when our fath-ers with

might-y en-deav-or se-cured all our

free-doms to-day, _____ that by their

might and by their right, it waves for-ev-er!

UNIT 4 REVIEW

Thinking About Words

Choose the word or words that best tells about each clue.

vote	government	President
monument	Congress	tax
White House	museum	laws
		citizen

1. The leader of our country

2. Where our country's leader lives

3. The group that makes our country's laws

4. What people do to choose leaders

5. Money that people pay to a community

6. A building or statue that honors someone

7. Where people go to look at interesting things

8. A group of people in charge of running a country, community, state, or city

9. Rules for a community, state, or country

10. A member of a community, state, or country

Thinking About Ideas

1. How does tax money help a community?

2. What are some rights that citizens have?

3. How can citizens get laws made or changed?

What would you like to ask a government leader?

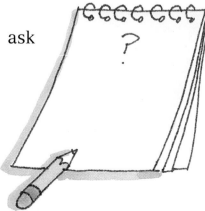

Using Skills

Reviewing Putting Things in Order

These pictures show how a flag is made.
Put the pictures in order.

1. Do you want to put these pictures in order by size or time?

2. Which picture will you put first?

3. Which picture will you put next?

4. Which picture comes last?

A

B

C

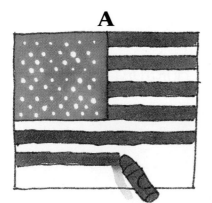
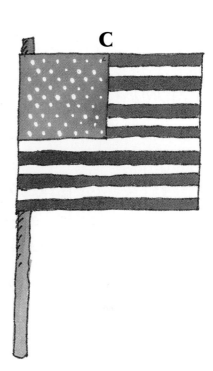

Make Your Own!

- Get three pieces of paper.
- Draw a picture of something that you did today on each piece of paper.
- Put the pictures in order by time.

Using Skills

Reviewing Using Time Lines

The time line shows some of the places where Jake went each day in Washington, D.C.

1. How many days does the time line show?

2. What did Jake visit on Monday?

3. Did he visit the Lincoln Memorial before or after the National Air and Space Museum?

Jake's Vacation

MONDAY	TUESDAY	WEDNESDAY	THURSDAY	FRIDAY
Washington Monument	Lincoln Memorial	National Museum of American History	National Air and Space Museum	White House

Unit Review Project

Make a Washington, D.C., Cup

- Draw a picture of your favorite monument or building in Washington, D.C., on colored paper.
- Cut out your picture and glue it onto a paper cup or can.
- Write one fact about the place on a piece of paper.
- Cut out the fact and glue it onto the back of the cup.
- Share your cup with a friend.

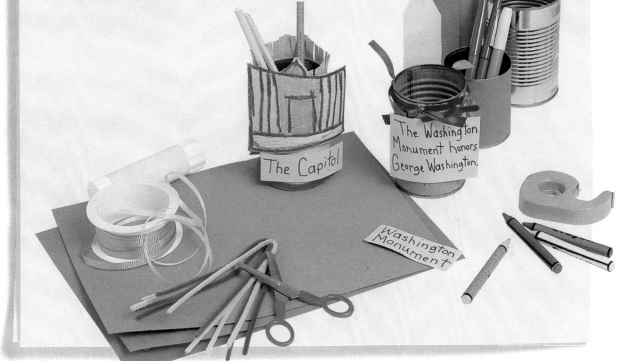

Reading on Your Own

You can look for these books at your library.

Key Words

explorer

colony

colonists

independence

slavery

pioneers

UNIT FIVE

Discovering Our Past

America's First People

Native Americans or Indians were the first people to live in America. They are part of our country's history. This map shows where some Native American groups lived in the past. Today Native Americans live in these and other places. Find the Yurok on the map.

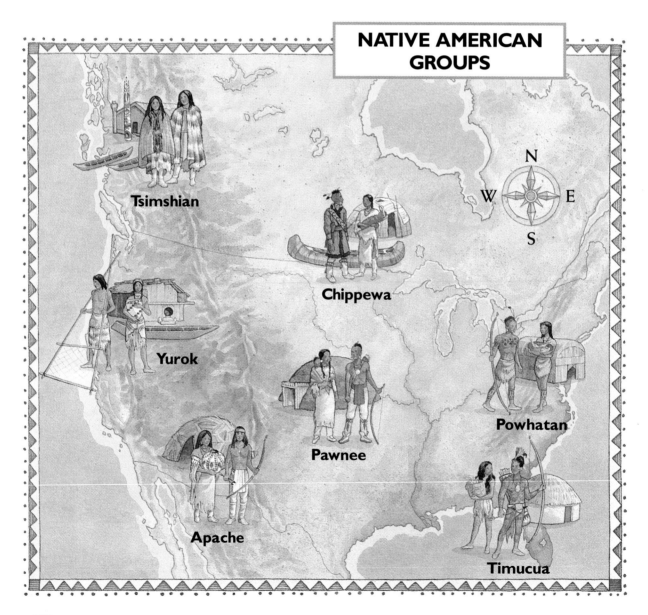

NATIVE AMERICAN GROUPS

Tsimshian

Chippewa

Yurok

Pawnee

Powhatan

Apache

Timucua

Will Chi–eri Carlson, Jr., is a Yurok. He lives in the state of California. In his language, Yurok means "downriver." The name tells where the Yurok lived along this river.

Will's home is near a special camp. It is a camp for Yurok boys and girls. The camp is where a Yurok village once stood long ago. Everyone takes a boat to get there.

At camp Will learned how the Yurok lived long ago. In the past, the Yurok got much of their food from the river. They fished in canoes cut from logs. They used nets like Will did to catch salmon.

Will played the Stick Game at camp. The Stick Game is a very old Yurok game. Boys play the game to build skills and to work out problems.

Will also learned about three dances. The Yurok danced them long ago and today. Each dance has a different purpose. This stick is used in the Jump Dance. It is danced to put order to the world.

Will had fun doing things as in the past. The camp helped him to see that the Yurok have a special history. He is happy to keep alive Native American ways.

1. Who were the first people to live in America?

2. How did Will learn about the past?

People Travel to America

Native Americans were the first people to live in America. Many years later other people came from Europe.

The first people to come from Europe to America were **explorers**. An explorer is a person who travels to a new place to learn about it.

The Vikings

Some of the first explorers from Europe were Vikings. The Viking explorers traveled in large wooden ships.

Another explorer from Europe was Christopher Columbus. He sailed to North America from Spain in 1492. Columbus was looking for a new way to get to the continent of Asia. He and his crew traveled in three ships called the *Niña,* the *Pinta,* and the *Santa María.* Find Columbus's route on the map.

Many other explorers followed Columbus. They hoped to find gold and other riches. They hoped to get land for their countries in Europe.

The Granger Collection

ATLANTIC OCEAN

EUROPE

Spain

NORTH AMERICA

AFRICA

West Indies

Route of Christopher Columbus

SOUTH AMERICA

After the explorers other people came to America from Europe. They came to live in **colonies**. A colony is a place that is ruled by another country. **Colonists** are people who live in a colony.

The first colonists from Europe came from the country of Spain. They built a colony called St. Augustine. At that time the land was home to the Timucua Indians. Today St. Augustine is part of the state of Florida.

One of the first buildings in St. Augustine was a fort. A fort is a very strong and safe building. Soldiers lived inside the fort's high walls.

Colonists lived on the land near the fort. Some were farmers. They planted grain and raised cattle. Other colonists earned a living by fishing. If you visit St. Augustine today, you can still see many of its old buildings.

1. What is the difference between an explorer and a colonist?

2. Would you have liked to have been an explorer? Why or why not?

GEOGRAPHY SKILLS
Using Grid Maps

Suppose you are visiting St. Augustine today. A grid map will help you find places.

Look at the grid map below. It is divided by lines that form squares. The squares have numbers and letters. You can use these to find places on the map.

All the squares in the first row across are **A**s. All the squares in the first row down are **1**s. So the first square in the top row is **A1**. What is the second square in the top row?

Put your finger on the square with a lake. Name this square by telling the letter and number of the square on the grid.

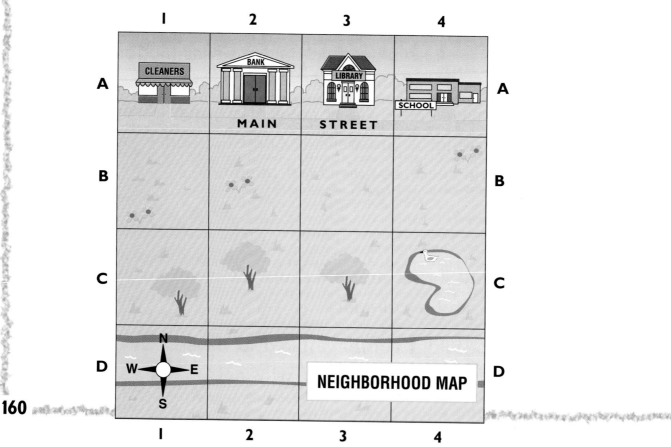

NEIGHBORHOOD MAP

Trying the Skill

Use this grid map to find places in St. Augustine.

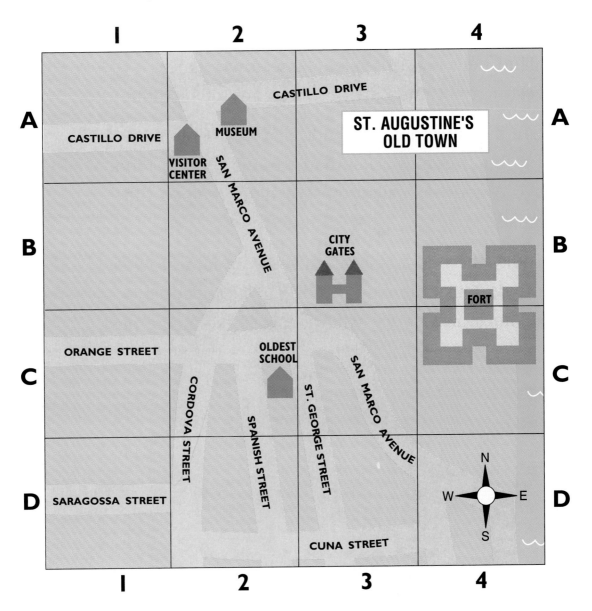

1. Look at A2. What buildings do you see?

2. What building is in C2?

3. Name the square that shows the City Gates. How did you know the name of the square?

4. When might you use a grid map?

A New Country

Soon colonists came to America from countries besides Spain. Colonists from the country of England built a place called Jamestown. Later, Jamestown became part of the colony of Virginia.

Life in Jamestown was not easy. The colonists had to build homes. They had trouble finding food. Native Americans called the Powhatan helped the colonists.

Today there is a special museum at Jamestown. The town looks the way it did long ago. People visit Jamestown to see what life was like in the past.

Another group of colonists from England was called the Pilgrims. They built a place called Plymouth. Later Plymouth became part of the colony of Massachussetts. Today Plymouth has a special museum like the one at Jamestown. At Plymouth you can see how the Pilgrims lived long ago.

More and more colonists came to America. Soon there were 13 English colonies all along the Atlantic Ocean. Find them on the map.

THE 13 ENGLISH COLONIES

NORTH AMERICA

MAINE
(part of Massachusetts)

NEW HAMPSHIRE

MASSACHUSETTS
•Plymouth

RHODE ISLAND

CONNECTICUT

NEW YORK

PENNSYLVANIA

NEW JERSEY

MARYLAND

DELAWARE

VIRGINIA
Jamestown•

NORTH CAROLINA

SOUTH CAROLINA

ATLANTIC OCEAN

GEORGIA

N W E S

The people in the 13 colonies had to follow the laws of England. Some colonists wanted the colonies to make their own laws. They wanted **independence** from England. Independence means to be free from other people or places.

On July 4, 1776, American leaders signed the Declaration of Independence. It said that Americans wanted to have a new country. It said that the colonies were "free and independent."

The king of England did not want Americans to be independent. America and England went to war. The war lasted many years. It was called the American Revolution.

An important American leader was George Washington. He led the American army.

George Washington said, "We are dreaming of independence and freedom." He helped the colonies win the war and their independence from England. After the war, he became the first President of the United States.

1. Why did Americans follow the laws of England for many years?

2. Why is the Declaration of Independence important to Americans?

STUDY SKILLS
Finding the Main Idea

Many people helped America to become free. One person was Paul Revere. He lived in the colony of Massachusetts. Read the paragraph below.

Paul Revere warned Americans to get ready for the British soldiers. One night Paul Revere got on his horse. He rode his horse from town to town. He shouted, "The British are coming! The British are coming!"

Most paragraphs have a main idea. A main idea tells what the paragraph is about. Look at the paragraph above. The sentence with the main idea has a line under it. What is the main idea? The other sentences in the paragraph tell more about the main idea. These sentences tell more about how Paul Revere warned the colonists.

Trying the Skill

There are many stories about Americans who helped our country to win its independence from England. Read this paragraph about another American who fought for freedom. Then answer the questions.

Molly Pitcher helped Americans to fight a battle against England. Molly Pitcher's husband was a soldier. When he got hurt, Molly Pitcher took his place. The other soldiers saw how brave Molly Pitcher was.

1. Which sentence tells the main idea of the paragraph?

2. Which sentences tell more about the main idea?

3. Why is it useful to know the main idea of a paragraph?

A Country at War

Americans fought to be free from England. But not all people living in America were free. The laws of the United States allowed slavery. Slavery is when one person owns another.

People from Africa were brought to America to be slaves. Slaves had no freedom. They were forced to work without pay. Many people tried to escape from slavery. Harriet Tubman was one person who escaped from slavery. Then she helped many other slaves to escape.

Harriet Tubman

When Abraham Lincoln was President, Americans fought in a war against each other. This war was called the Civil War. One of the reasons for the Civil War was slavery. President Lincoln helped to end slavery. After the war was over, slavery was against the law.

?

1. What happened after the Civil War?

2. How is the life of a person in slavery different from the life of a free person?

The Country Grows

Over the years, more people came to live in the United States. At first, many people lived in the East. As the East got crowded, people moved to less crowded places. These people were called **pioneers**. Pioneers are people who lead the way into a land that they do not know.

The map on the next page shows some of the trails that the pioneers followed to the west. The pioneers also came north from Mexico.

All of these new people were looking for land where they could live. But most of this land was already the home of Native Americans. In some places Native Americans fought against soldiers to keep their land. But the pioneers kept coming.

Before long, Native Americans had lost most of their land to the pioneers. Many Native Americans were forced to move to other places. Other Native Americans had to share the land with the pioneers.

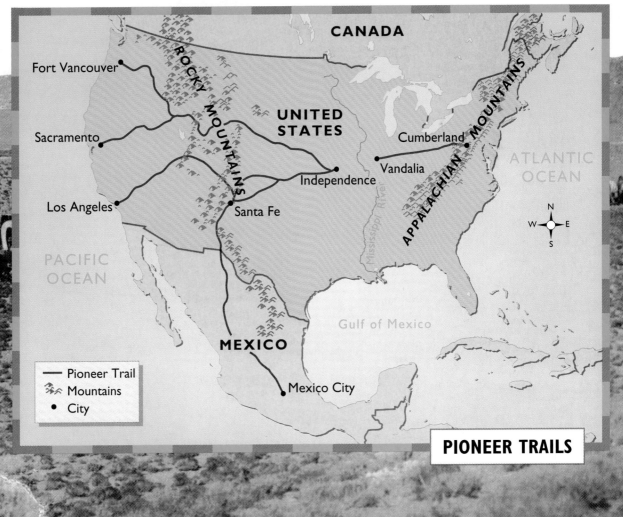

PIONEER TRAILS

Today the United States is still growing.
Many people still come to the United States
from other countries. These newcomers
bring different languages. They also bring
different clothing, music, and dances.

Many groups bring special foods and ways of cooking to our country. What foods can you name that come from other countries?

1. Why did some people move west?

2. How do people from other countries add to life in the United States?

Kansas City

MISSOURI

Caring About Kansas City

Jessica Ayers is in Mrs. Lerner's class at the Red Bridge School. Her school is in Kansas City in the state of Missouri.

One year Mrs. Lerner's class joined the fight to save Union Station. This was an old train station. It was not used anymore. Many people worried it would be torn down.

The class recorded a song about saving Union Station. It was played on radio stations all over the city. They also gave tours of the station. They showed visitors that Union Station was a special building. It was important to the history of Kansas City.

In 1994 the city found a new owner for Union Station. Workers began fixing it up.

Mrs. Lerner's class made a calendar. They put in drawings of people who helped save the station. Jessica Ayers drew pictures for the calendar. She said, "Our calendar says thank you to the people who work hard to make Kansas City a better place."

Mrs. Lerner's class makes calendars every year. They draw pictures of special people and places in their community. When the calendars are finished, the class gives them to family, friends, and city leaders.

UNION STATION SONG
Words and Music by Barbara Katz

How
My
Family
Lives
in
America

Susan Kuklin

from

How My Family Lives in America

by Susan Kuklin

欽
Admire

蘭
Orchid

My name in America is April. I also have a Chinese name: *Chin* (ching), which means "admire" and *Lan* (lan), which means "orchid."

Both my parents are Chinese and were born in Taiwan. Taiwan is an island on the other side of the world.

My papa came to New York without his parents to go to school and my mama moved here with her family. Because Julius, my older brother, and May, my older sister, and I were born in America, we are called Chinese Americans.

There are many Chinese Americans. But we do not all speak the same Chinese language. The way my family speaks Chinese is called Mandarin.

In Mandarin, I call my daddy *baba* (bah-bah) and my mommy *mama* (mah-mah). It sounds something like English, but when we write the words they look very different. Another thing that's different in Chinese is that words aren't made with letters. Each word has its own special marks.

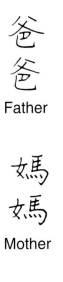

爸爸
Father

媽媽
Mother

During the week we go to public school, but on Saturday we go to Chinese school. There we learn how to speak and write in Chinese, like my parents learned in Taiwan. When I write English letters, I write from the left side of the page to the right. When I write in Chinese, I write from the right to the left. And I write in rows from the top of the page to the bottom. For us Chinese-American kids there are many things to remember.

In Chinese school we also learn a special kind of writing called calligraphy. We use a brush instead of a pen, black ink, and special paper made from stalks of rice. Our teacher shows us the right way to hold the brush.

芝
蔴
涼
麵

Cold Sesame
Noodles

My favorite part of Chinese school is snack time. Today, Mama made me cold sesame noodles, *tsu ma liang mein* (tsu mah leeang mee-en). I eat them with a fork, but most Chinese people eat their noodles with chopsticks. I'm just learning to eat with chopsticks.

Papa told us that an Italian explorer named Marco Polo discovered noodles in China a long time ago and introduced them to his country.

When Mama brought home takeout, Julius asked if a Chinese explorer discovered pizza in Italy.

Mama and Papa laughed and said, "No."

While we eat our pizza we play a game to test our wits. Papa asks us to look for letters hidden in the picture on the pizza box. Julius sees a *V* in the pizza man's shoe. May finds an *L*.

Oh, look! I can even see the Chinese letter *Ba* (bah), in the pizza man's eyebrows. *Ba* means "eight" in Chinese.

Eight

七
巧
板

Chi chiao
bang

At night when we have finished all our chores and all our homework, we play *Chi chiao bang* (chee chow bang). In America some people call it Tangram. This is a popular game in Taiwan, like checkers is in America. My grandparents and even my great-grandparents played this game.

To play, you move seven different shapes to build a new shape. I like to make a pussycat. It is very difficult, but I can do it. Papa says, "Go slowly and think about a cat. After a while your mind will start to run and you will see the cat in the shapes." He's right.

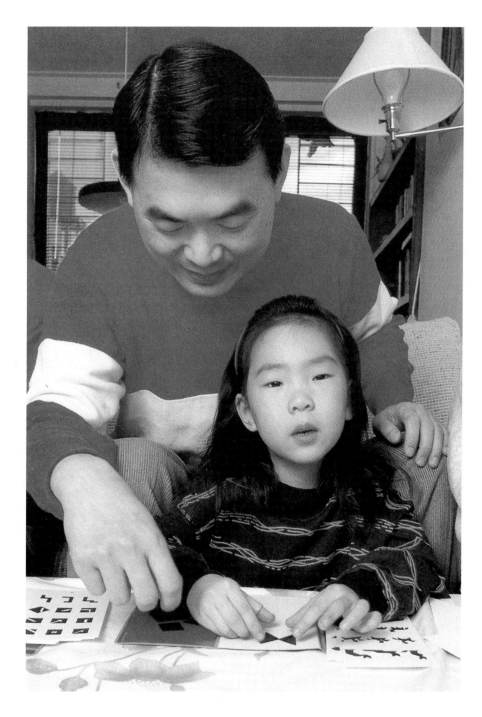

There is an old Chinese saying, "The older you are the wiser you become." When I become a grown-up, I will remember to tell this to my family.

UNIT 5 REVIEW

Thinking About Words

Choose one word in the box to answer each question.

pioneers	**colonists**	**colonies**
slavery	**explorers**	**independence**

1. Who traveled to learn about new places?

2. Who came to America to live in places ruled by another country?

3. What did Americans want from England?

4. What did Harriet Tubman help people escape from?

5. Who led the way into land that they did not know?

6. What are places that are ruled by another land called?

Thinking About Ideas

1. Who were the first people to live in America?

2. How is an explorer different from a colonist?

3. What could you learn by visiting St. Augustine?

4. Why did the colonists fight against the English?

5. What was one reason for the Civil War?

6. How did pioneers cause problems for Native Americans?

SHARE WITH A FRIEND

Suppose you could live in a time long ago. When would it be? What would your life be like?

184

Using Skills

Reviewing Using Grid Maps

1. In what square did Paul Revere begin his ride?

2. What town is in square C4?

3. What town is in square A4?

4. In what square did Paul Revere end his ride?

5. What is the town where the ride ended?

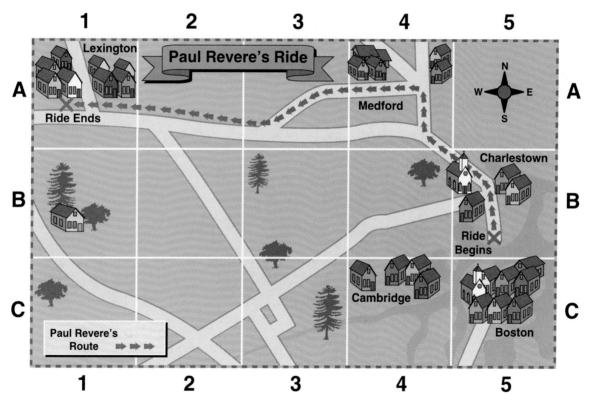

Make Your Own!

- Draw a grid on a piece of paper.
- Write letters by the squares on the sides of the grid.
- Write numbers by the squares at the top and bottom of the grid.
- Draw a treasure map on the grid.
- Have others ask questions about the grid map.

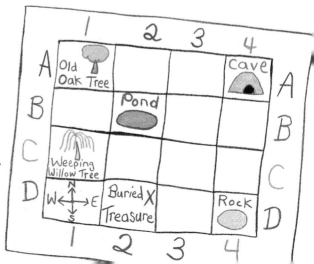

Using Skills

Reviewing Finding the Main Idea

Read this paragraph about a pioneer boy.

> My family moved west when I was eight years old. We packed all of our things in a big wagon. We traveled for six months. It was a hard but exciting trip.

1. Which sentence tells the main idea of the paragraph?

2. Why is it important to know the main idea of the paragraph?

3. What do the other sentences tell about the main idea?

UNIT REVIEW PROJECT

Make a History Pictures Time Line

- List three things that happened in this unit.
- Draw pictures of these things on different pieces of colored paper.
- Write a sentence that tells about each thing.
- Have a partner put your pictures in order.
- Punch a hole in the top of each picture.
- Hang your pictures on a piece of string.

Reading on Your Own

You can look for these books at your library.

UNIT SIX

People, Places, and Holidays

Key Words

celebrate

holiday

custom

Special Americans

Meet Barbara and her friends Andy, Mark, and Judy. They are putting on a play. The play is about special Americans from long ago and today.

Hello!
My name is
George Washington.
I was the first President of the United States. I helped to write the Constitution.

Greetings!
My name is
Benjamin Franklin.
I also helped to write the Constitution. I was a writer, a scientist, and an inventor. An inventor makes useful things for people.

George Washington

Benjamin Franklin

My name is Daniel Boone. I explored Kentucky before it was a state. I made trails for others to follow. Later, I helped to start a town called Boonesboro.

Hello. I'm Sojourner Truth. I was once a slave. Later I spoke out against slavery. I helped people who escaped from slavery to find homes. I also worked for women to have more rights.

Daniel Boone

Sojourner Truth

Hello.
I'm Abraham Lincoln.
I was born in a log cabin. I read books whenever I got the chance. I was the President of the United States during the Civil War.

My name is Clara Barton. I was a nurse who helped soldiers during the Civil War. I also started the American Red Cross. It still helps people today.

Clara Barton

Abraham Lincoln

I am
Mary McLeod Bethune.
I was a teacher who started
a school for African American
students. I worked to make
life better for all Americans.

My name is Chief Joseph.
I was a leader of the Nez Percé
Indians. The United States
government wanted the land
where we lived. We fought to
stay on the land, but
lost the fight.

Chief Joseph

Mary McLeod Bethune

I am Martin Luther King, Jr. I worked for the rights of African Americans. I hoped that one day all people would get along with each other.

My name is César Chávez. I worked to get better pay for farm workers. I tried to make sure that all farm workers were treated fairly.

Martin Luther King, Jr.

César Chávez

Maya Lin

My name is Maya Lin. I made the plans for the Vietnam Veterans Memorial. It honors Americans who fought in the Vietnam War.

Hello. I am Sandra Day O'Connor. I am the first woman ever to serve as a judge on the Supreme Court of the United States. A judge makes decisions about law.

Sandra Day O'Connor

Now the play is over. Which other special Americans would you like to learn more about in a play?

1. Tell why one person in this lesson is a special American.

2. How are the Americans in this lesson alike? How are they different?

THINKING SKILLS
Making Predictions

You can make **predictions** when you read. When you make a prediction, you tell what comes next. A prediction is based on what you already know plus what you have just read. Read the paragraph below to make a prediction about what happened next.

Thomas Edison was an inventor. In his time people used lamps lit by gas. Thomas Edison thought he could make a better light using electricity.

How could you make a prediction about what Thomas Edison did next? You know that Thomas Edison thought he could make a better light. You know that there are electric lights today. Did you make a prediction that Thomas Edison invented a new way to get light? That is just what he did. He invented an electric light bulb that everyone could use.

Trying the Skill

Read the paragraph below about Thomas Edison. Then answer the questions.

In Thomas Edison's time, no machines could play back sound. People had no way to put voices on a machine. If people wanted to hear music, they had to hear it in person. Thomas Edison thought he could do something about this.

1. What ways can we hear music today?

2. What prediction did you make about what Thomas Edison did? Why?

3. How could making predictions about something help you?

Special Places in Our Country

Barbara and her friends had fun putting on their play about special Americans. Now Barbara and Mark are making a map.

"This map shows special places in our country. Some places are outdoors," says Barbara. "I drew one of the tallest trees in the world. It's a redwood tree. You can see them in Redwood National Park in California."

Barbara picks up an orange crayon. "I'm drawing the Grand Canyon in Arizona," she says. "A canyon is a very, very deep valley."

"I drew the Mississippi River," says Mark. "It's one of the longest rivers in our country! Now I'm drawing the Everglades in Florida. Many different plants and animals live there, including alligators and big turtles."

"The map also shows special things that people built," says Barbara. "This is the Golden Gate Bridge in San Francisco, California. It is like a big gate to the city."

"I drew a fort called The Alamo," says Mark. "It's in San Antonio, Texas. Long ago a big battle took place there. The people of Texas fought to be free from Mexico. People still say, 'Remember The Alamo!'"

"This place helps us to remember the pioneers," says Barbara. "It is called the Gateway Arch and is in St. Louis, Missouri. Many pioneers began their trip west in St. Louis. So this city is called the 'Gateway to the West.'"

"I drew the Statue of Liberty in New York City, New York," says Mark. "It's a symbol of freedom. It stands for the many people who came to our country looking for better lives."

Barbara and Mark liked making a map of special places in our country. Find the places that they drew on their map.

Special Places in Our Country

1. Tell why one of the places in this lesson is special to Americans.

2. Into what groups could you sort the places in this lesson?

STUDY SKILLS
Using Bar Graphs

Barbara's family took a trip. The bar graph shows how much time they spent in four special places. A bar graph is a graph that uses bars to show the number of things.

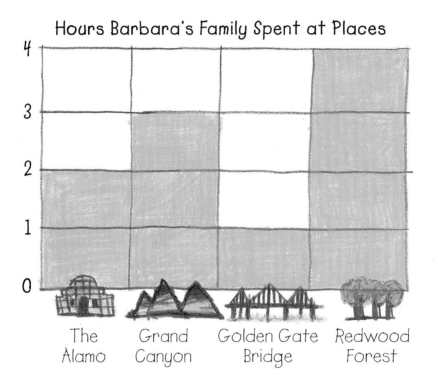

Hours Barbara's Family Spent at Places

The Alamo   Grand Canyon   Golden Gate Bridge   Redwood Forest

To use a bar graph, first read the title. The title of the bar graph above is "Hours Barbara's Family Spent at Places." The bottom of this graph names places Barbara's family visited. The side of the graph shows the number of hours. Each bar tells how many hours the family spent at each place. Move your finger up the bar for The Alamo. It ends at the number 2. That means her family spent 2 hours at The Alamo. How much time did they spend at the Grand Canyon?

Trying the Skill

Mark and his family also visited many of our country's special places. Read the bar graph below to answer the questions.

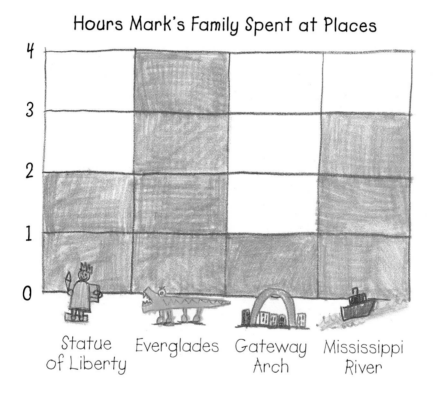

Hours Mark's Family Spent at Places

Statue of Liberty Everglades Gateway Arch Mississippi River

1. How many places did Mark and his family visit?

2. How much time did Mark and his family spend at the Gateway Arch?

3. Did Mark and his family spend more time at the Everglades or the Mississippi River? How do you know?

4. When might you use a bar graph? Why?

Special Holidays

Barbara and her family **celebrate** special days. To celebrate means to honor a special day by doing something special. Special days are also called **holidays**.

Many holidays are in the winter. Christmas is celebrated on December 25. Barbara and her family give each other gifts under their Christmas tree.

Three Kings Day is celebrated on January 6. Andy and his family celebrate this holiday by giving each other gifts and seeing a parade.

Hanukkah is usually celebrated in December. This holiday lasts for eight days. Mark and his family light a candle each day. They also give each other gifts.

Kwanzaa lasts for seven days from December 26 to January 1. Each day Judy and her family light a candle. They eat special foods and children receive gifts.

?

1. How are the holidays in this lesson alike? How are they different?

2. Name a holiday that people celebrate in your community. Tell how it is celebrated.

Celebrating in Many Countries

People celebrate all around the world. One holiday that people celebrate in the United States is New Year's Day. Barbara sees that this is the first day of the year on her calendar.

On New Year's Day, it is the **custom** for many Americans to go to parties and spend time with family and friends. A custom is a special way that a group of people does something. On New Year's Day some Americans make a list of things they plan to do differently in the new year. This is also a custom.

In Quebec, Canada, people enjoy a winter celebration for more than a week. One custom is a big parade on the first day of the celebration. Another custom is for a large snowman with a red cap to greet visitors.

There is also a winter celebration in Sapporo, Japan. People use the winter snow and ice to carve beautiful things. People also enjoy winter sports.

People around the world celebrate many summer holidays. In Oaxaca, Mexico, people celebrate "Mondays on the Hill." Some people dance at a special place on a hilltop. Many others watch the dancers.

During late summer, some people in Ghana have a food celebration. It is the custom for people to give food to anyone who visits their home.

Mexico

Ghana

Warm summer weather does not last long in some countries. So people in these places celebrate with a holiday. It happens on the longest day of the year.

In Norway people dress in clothes like those worn long ago. Children celebrate with a parade. What days do you like to celebrate?

Norway

1. Tell how one holiday in this lesson is celebrated.

2. What holiday customs do you know about?

CITIZENSHIP
Making a Difference

NEW YORK

New York City

Celebrating Together

"Come to our party," says second grader Anita Hernandez. "You will learn a lot and have fun too."

Each year in May the children at P.S. 112 hold a big celebration. P.S. 112 is in New York City in the state of New York. Over 300 people come to the celebration. They sing and dance. They listen to poems and stories about Mexico. They also watch a fashion show.

The celebration is Cinco de Mayo. On this day people share the customs of Mexico. The holiday celebrates a special day in May long ago. On that day people from Mexico fought for their freedom.

The parents at P.S. 112 dress up the school with flags, posters, and paper flowers. Others help, too. Mrs. Carmen Morales is a grandparent of one of the children at the school. She likes to help and learn about Mexican ways.

Anita is in the fashion show of Mexican clothing with her mother. She wears a dress her mother made. After the show, people eat Mexican food made by the parents. Anita brings sope, a tortilla with beans and cheese. "Try it, you'll like it!" she says.

Everyone enjoys the celebration. Mrs. Morales says, "It makes people feel good to share their holidays with others."

Celebrating in the U.S.A.

Barbara and her friends celebrate days that are important to them. They also celebrate days that are important to all Americans.

Barbara's first day of school is after the holiday of Labor Day. Labor is another word for work. On Labor Day we honor all the people in our country who work. There are many parades on Labor Day to show how workers have made our country strong.

SCHOOLS

BLUE COLLAR

HOSPITALS

HEALTH WORKERS

0,000 New Yorkers Serving NEW YORK

DIS COU

The Granger Collection

In November Americans celebrate Thanksgiving. This holiday helps us to remember a special celebration held long ago by the Pilgrims.

The Pilgrims had a very hard time in their first year in America. But Native Americans called the Wampanoag helped them. At the end of the year the Pilgrims wanted to give thanks to God. They had a big feast. They invited their friends the Wampanoag and thanked them for their help.

We celebrate the birthdays of some special Americans during the winter. Martin Luther King, Jr., was born in January. We honor him on Martin Luther King, Jr., Day. Americans remember his work to help all Americans be treated fairly.

George Washington and Abraham Lincoln were both born in February. We honor these two Presidents on Presidents' Day.

In the spring we celebrate Memorial Day. On this day in May Americans honor soldiers who died fighting for our country.

The Fourth of July is a favorite summer holiday. This important holiday is also called Independence Day. It reminds us that the Declaration of Independence was signed on July 4, 1776. On that day our country became the United States of America. This holiday is often called our country's birthday.

On July 4 many Americans go to see a parade. They celebrate being Americans. They are proud to live in the United States of America.

1. Name one of our country's holidays and tell why it is important.

2. Look at a calendar. What is our country's next holiday? Predict how your class will celebrate the holiday.

This Land Is Your Land

Words and Music
by Woody Guthrie

Chorus

This land is your land, _____ This land is my land, _____

from Cal - i - for - nia _____ to the New York is - land, _____

From the red-wood for - est _____ to the Gulf Stream wa - ters; _____

This land was made for you and me. _____

Verse

C

As I was walk-ing _____ that rib-bon of high - way, _____

D7

G

I saw a-bove me _____ that end-less sky - way. _____

C

G

I saw be - low me _____ that gold-en val - ley,

D7

G **Repeat Chorus**

This land was made for you and me. _____

UNIT 6 REVIEW

Thinking About Words

Choose the best word to fill each blank.

celebrate	custom	holiday

1. My favorite _____ is Thanksgiving Day.
2. Our class decided to _____ the first day of spring with a picnic.
3. It is the _____ to blow out candles on a birthday cake.

Thinking About Ideas

1. Name two famous Americans who helped people in our country.
2. Why might people visit the Everglades?
3. Why is the Statue of Liberty important to Americans?
4. What is one way that people celebrate in another country?
5. Why do we celebrate Thanksgiving?
6. Why is the Fourth of July often called our country's birthday?

SHARE WITH A FRIEND

Think about your favorite holiday. Tell a friend how you celebrate it.

Using Skills

Reviewing Using Bar Graphs

1. What is the title of the bar graph?

2. How many students told stories about Presidents' Day?

3. Which holiday had two stories?

4. Did more students tell stories about Thanksgiving Day or about Independence Day?

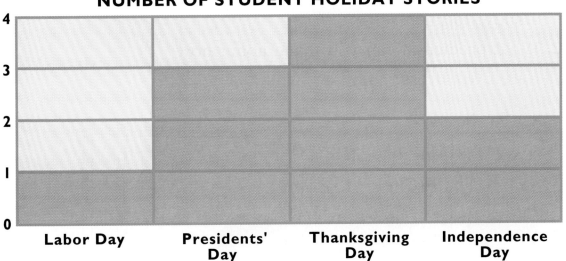

NUMBER OF STUDENT HOLIDAY STORIES

Labor Day   Presidents' Day   Thanksgiving Day   Independence Day

Make Your Own!

- Copy the bar graph shown.
- Fill in the bar graph to show how many days long each holiday is.

NUMBER OF DAYS EACH HOLIDAY LASTS

Christmas   Hanukkah   Kwanzaa   Three Kings Day

Using Skills

Reviewing Making Predictions

Read the paragraph.

It was morning. Karen turned on the radio. A weatherperson said a snowstorm was coming. Karen opened the closet. She thought about which clothes to wear.

1. What do you know about dressing for a snowstorm?

2. What prediction can you make about how Karen will dress?

UNIT REVIEW PROJECT

Make a Holiday Calendar

- On a large piece of paper draw a blank calendar for the month that has your favorite holiday.
- Write the month at the top of the calendar.
- Write a number in each box.
- Write the holiday in the correct box.
- Fill in the calendar with holiday pictures.

Reading on Your Own

You can look for these books at your library.

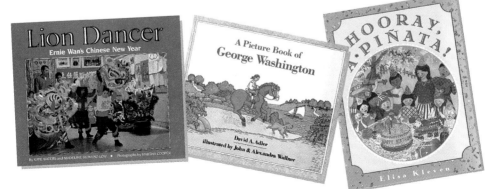

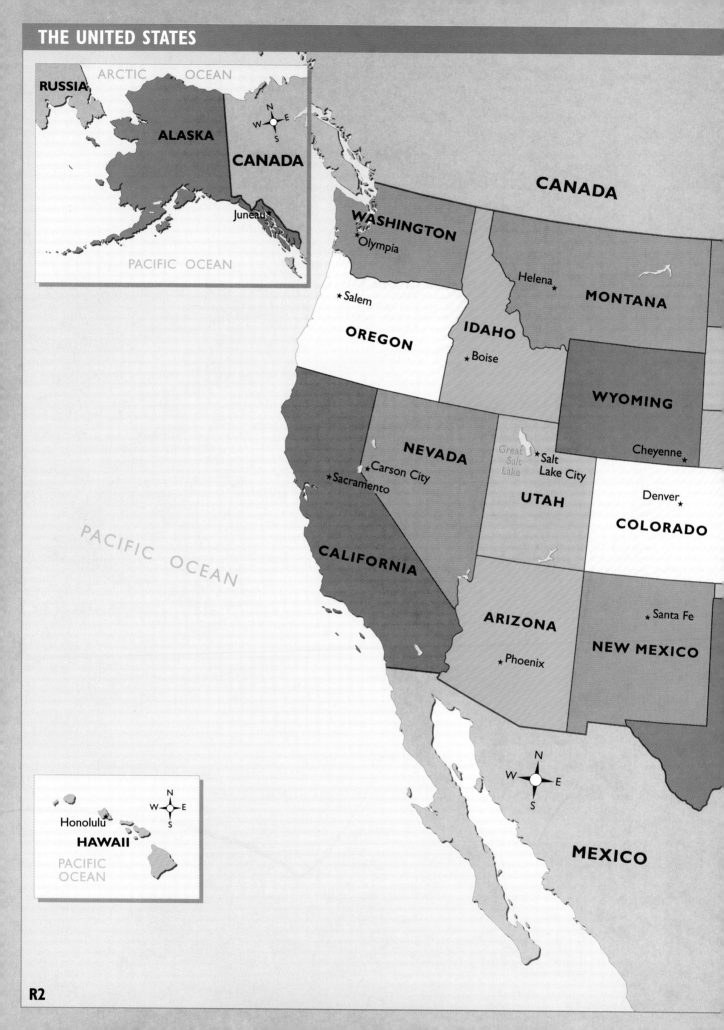

ARCTIC OCEAN

RUSSIA

ALASKA

CANADA

Juneau★

PACIFIC OCEAN

CANADA

WASHINGTON

Olympia

Salem★

OREGON

IDAHO

Boise★

Helena★

MONTANA

WYOMING

Cheyenne★

NEVADA

Carson City★

Sacramento★

Great Salt Lake

Salt Lake City★

UTAH

Denver★

COLORADO

PACIFIC OCEAN

CALIFORNIA

ARIZONA

Phoenix★

Santa Fe★

NEW MEXICO

Honolulu★

HAWAII

PACIFIC OCEAN

MEXICO

CANADA

NORTH DAKOTA
★ Bismarck

SOUTH DAKOTA
★ Pierre

MINNESOTA
St. Paul ★

Lake Superior

MICHIGAN

WISCONSIN
Madison ★

Lake Michigan

Lake Huron

Lansing ★

NEBRASKA
Lincoln ★

IOWA
★ Des Moines

ILLINOIS
Springfield ★

INDIANA
Indianapolis ★

Lake Erie

OHIO
Columbus ★

VERMONT
Montpelier ★

MAINE
Augusta ★

NEW HAMPSHIRE
Concord ★

Lake Ontario

NEW YORK
Albany ★

MASSACHUSETTS
Boston ★
Providence ★

Hartford ★
CONNECTICUT

RHODE ISLAND

PENNSYLVANIA
Harrisburg ★

Trenton ★
NEW JERSEY

Dover ★
DELAWARE
MARYLAND

Annapolis ★
Washington, D.C. ⊛

KANSAS
Topeka ★

MISSOURI
Jefferson City ★

KENTUCKY
Frankfort ★

WEST VIRGINIA
Charleston ★

VIRGINIA
Richmond ★

OKLAHOMA
★ Oklahoma City

ARKANSAS
Little Rock ★

TENNESSEE
Nashville ★

NORTH CAROLINA
Raleigh ★

SOUTH CAROLINA
Columbia ★

ATLANTIC OCEAN

TEXAS
Austin ★

MISSISSIPPI
Jackson ★

LOUISIANA
Baton Rouge ★

ALABAMA
Montgomery ★

GEORGIA
★ Atlanta

Tallahassee ★

FLORIDA

Gulf of Mexico

THE BAHAMAS

⊛ National capital   ★ State capital

CUBA

R3

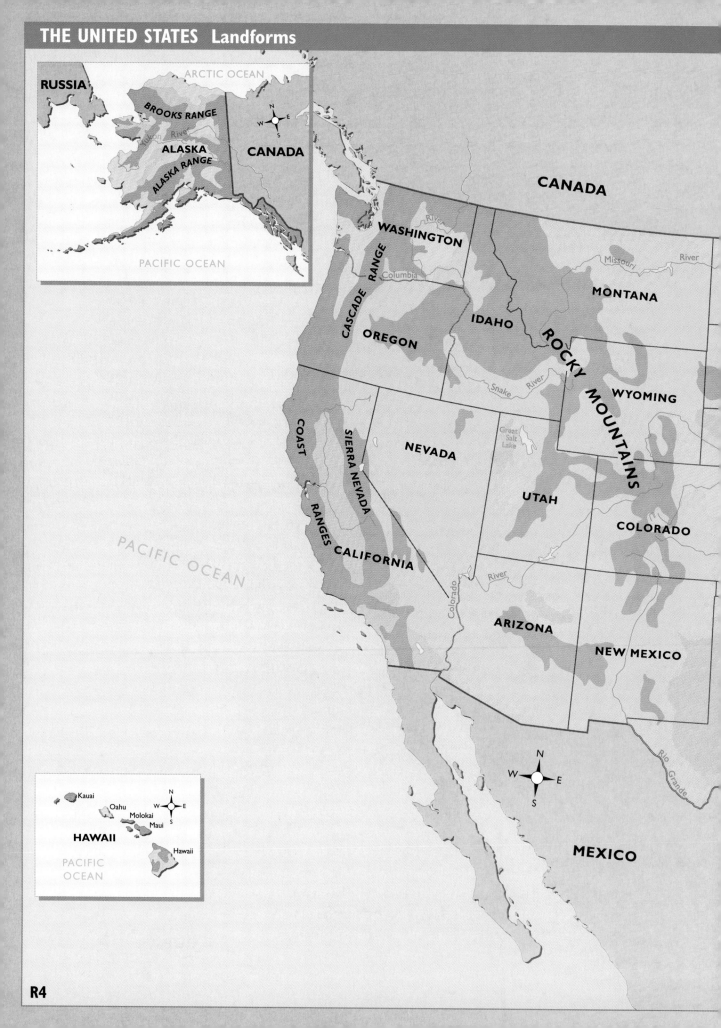

RUSSIA

ARCTIC OCEAN

BROOKS RANGE

ALASKA

ALASKA RANGE

CANADA

PACIFIC OCEAN

Yukon River

CANADA

WASHINGTON

River

CASCADE RANGE

Columbia

OREGON

IDAHO

Missouri

River

MONTANA

ROCKY MOUNTAINS

WYOMING

Snake River

COAST

SIERRA NEVADA

NEVADA

Great Salt Lake

UTAH

PACIFIC OCEAN

RANGES CALIFORNIA

Colorado

COLORADO

River

ARIZONA

NEW MEXICO

Colorado

Kauai

Oahu

Molokai

Maui

HAWAII

Hawaii

PACIFIC OCEAN

Rio Grande

MEXICO

CANADA

MAINE

VERMONT NEW
HAMPSHIRE

MASSACHUSETTS

CONNECTICUT

RHODE
ISLAND

NEW YORK

NEW JERSEY

DELAWARE

MARYLAND

PENNSYLVANIA

MOUNTAINS

Washington,
D.C.

VIRGINIA

WEST
VIRGINIA

COASTAL

PLAIN

NORTH
CAROLINA

APPALACHIAN

KENTUCKY

SOUTH
CAROLINA

TENNESSEE

ATLANTIC OCEAN

ATLANTIC

GEORGIA

ALABAMA

MISSISSIPPI

COASTAL

PLAIN

LOUISIANA

FLORIDA

THE
BAHAMAS

TEXAS

GULF

Gulf of Mexico

CUBA

NORTH
DAKOTA

MINNESOTA

WISCONSIN

MICHIGAN

Lake Superior

Lake Michigan

Lake Huron

Lake Ontario

Lake Erie

SOUTH
DAKOTA

IOWA

ILLINOIS

INDIANA

OHIO

Wabash River

River

Ohio

NEBRASKA

Platte River

GREAT

PLAINS

Missouri

River

KANSAS

MISSOURI

OZARK

PLATEAU

Arkansas

River

Red

OKLAHOMA

ARKANSAS

Mississippi

River

Tennessee

Savannah River

Mississippi

River

Legend:
- Mountains
- Hills
- Plains
- ✵ National capital

R5

ARCTIC OCEAN

NORTH
AMERICA

ATLANTIC
OCEAN

PACIFIC   OCEAN

SOUTH
AMERICA

ANTARCTICA

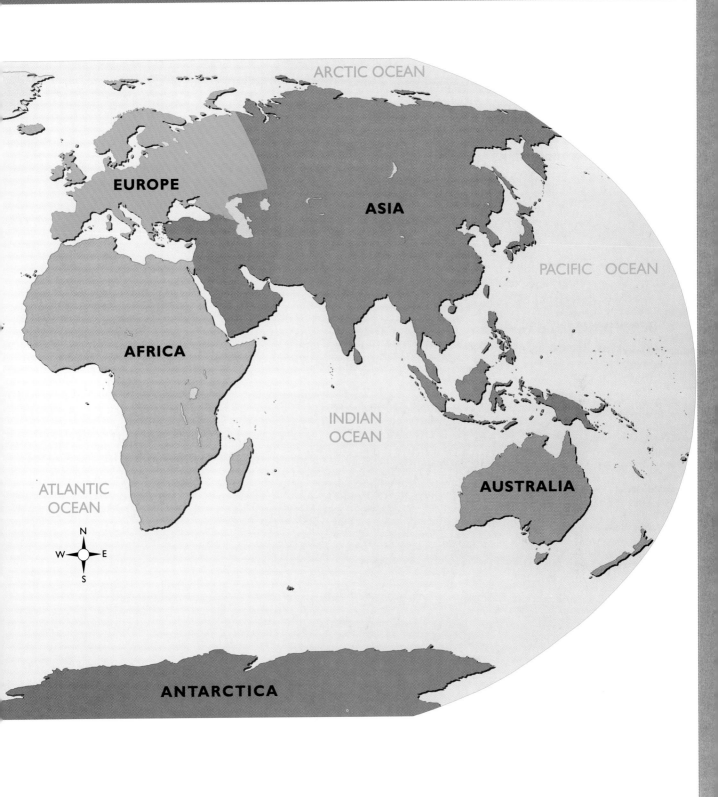

Dictionary of GEOGRAPHIC WORDS

HILL Land that is higher than the land around it, but lower than a mountain.

PENINSULA Land that has water on three sides.

PLAIN Flat land.

LAKE Body of water with land all around it.

ISLAND Land that has water all around it.

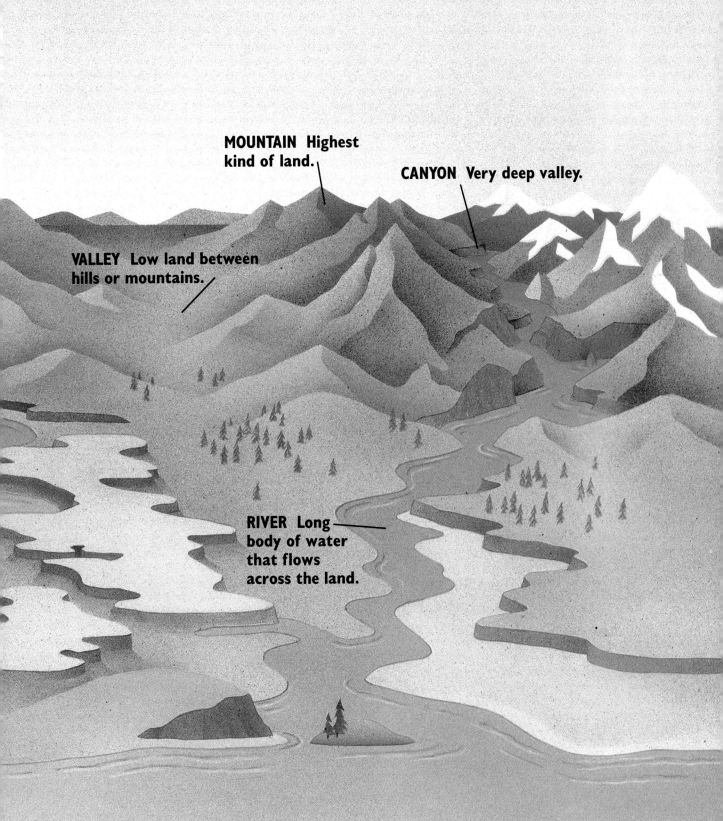

MOUNTAIN Highest kind of land.

CANYON Very deep valley.

VALLEY Low land between hills or mountains.

RIVER Long body of water that flows across the land.

OCEAN Very large body of salt water.

PICTURE GLOSSARY

alike Things that are the same in some way. These houses look **alike**. (page 12)

ancestor A relative who lived before you were born. My **ancestors** came to America over 100 years ago. (page 9)

bar graph A graph with bars showing the number of things. Sue's **bar graph** shows how many books she read. (page 202)

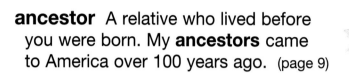

NUMBER OF BOOKS SUE READ

WEEK 1   WEEK 2   WEEK 3   WEEK 4

calendar A chart that shows the months, weeks, and days of the year. January is the first month on the **calendar**. (page 22)

capital A city where leaders of a state work. Salem is the **capital** of Oregon. (page 40)

★ Salem

OREGON

celebrate To honor a special day by doing something special. I **celebrate** my birthday with a birthday cake. (page 204)

citizen A member of a country, state, or community. We are proud to be American **citizens**. (page 118)

colonist A person who lives in a colony. The **colonists** came from England to live in Jamestown. (page 158)

colony A place that is ruled by another country. Virginia was once a **colony** of England. (page 158)

community A place that has many different neighborhoods. My **community** has a playground. (page 16)

compass rose Shows directions on a map. I can find north with this **compass rose**. (page 44)

Congress Part of our country's government. **Congress** works in the Capitol Building. (page 137)

continent A very large body of land. There are seven **continents** on Earth. (page G8)

country A land and the people who live there. Canada is a **country** north of the United States. (page G7)

custom The special way a group of people does things. A Fourth of July parade is a **custom**. (page 206)

different Things that are not the same. These kites have **different** colors. (page 12)

directions North, east, south, and west. There are four main **directions** on Earth. (page G9)

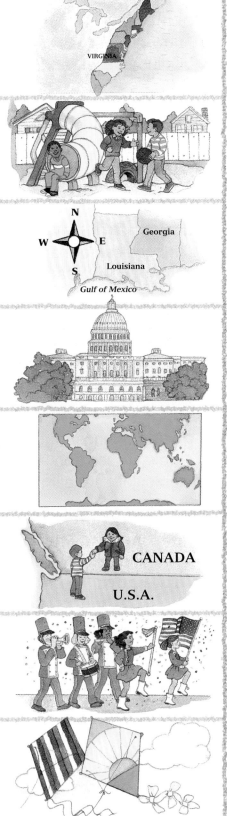

explorer A person who travels to a new place to learn about it. Christopher Columbus was an **explorer**. (page 156)

factory A building where things are made. The people in this **factory** make computers. (page 94)

flow chart Shows the order in which things flow, or happen. This **flow chart** shows how bread is made. (page 86)

globe A model of Earth. This **globe** shows continents and oceans. (page G8)

goods Things that people make or grow. These apples, the table, and the tablecloth are all **goods**. (page 82)

government The group of people who run a community, state, or country. Our city's **government** makes laws. (page 126)

grid map A map divided by lines that form squares used to find places. This is a **grid map** of a town. (page 160)

hill Land that is higher than land around it, but lower than a mountain. Our house is on a **hill**. (page 55)

history The story of the past. There are many books about our country's **history**. (page 4)

holiday A special day. Thanksgiving Day is a **holiday**. (page 204)

independence To be free from other people or places. Americans won **independence** from England. (page 164)

island Land that has water all around it. There is a tree on the **island**. (page 56)

lake A body of water with land all around it. We go swimming in the **lake**. (page 53)

landform A kind of land, such as a plain, hill, or mountain. Mountains are the highest kind of **landform**. (page 58)

law A rule for a community, state, or country. Obey the **law** and cross the street at a green light. (page 119)

main idea Tells what a story or a paragraph is about. Sometimes the **main idea** is a sentence in a story. (page 166)

map A drawing of a place. This is a **map** of New Mexico. (page G4)

Santa Fe
★
NEW MEXICO

map key Tells what the symbols on a map stand for. In this **map key** a tree stands for a park. (page G5)

Map Key
Park
House
School

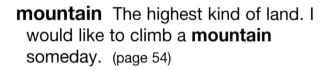

monument A building or statue that honors a person or something that happened. This **monument** honors Abraham Lincoln. (page 133)

mountain The highest kind of land. I would like to climb a **mountain** someday. (page 54)

museum A place where people go to look at interesting things. Our class visited a history **museum**. (page 135)

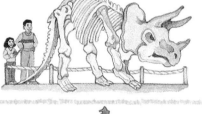

natural resource Something in nature that people use. This tree is a **natural resource**. (page 60)

needs Things people must have in order to live. My **needs** are food, clothes, shelter, and love. (page 104)

neighborhood A place where people live, work, and play. There is a park in my **neighborhood**. (page 15)

ocean A very large body of salt water. The Pacific Ocean is the largest **ocean** in the world. (page G8)

peninsula Land that has water on three sides. The state of Florida is a **peninsula**. (page 56)

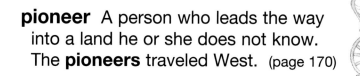

pioneer A person who leads the way into a land he or she does not know. The **pioneers** traveled West. (page 170)

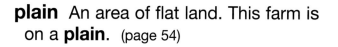

plain An area of flat land. This farm is on a **plain**. (page 54)

prediction To tell what might happen. James made a **prediction** that the blue team would win. (page 196)

President The most important leader of our country. Abraham Lincoln was our 16th **President**. (page 132)

relative A person who belongs to the same family as someone else. My cousins Jane and Martha are my favorite **relatives**. (page 8)

river A long body of water that flows across the land. This **river** is very wide. (page 53)

route A way of going from one place to another. This map shows a **route** to the beach. (page 92)

service Something useful that people do for others. Teaching is an important **service** job. (page 84)

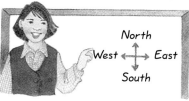

PICTURE GLOSSARY

shelter A place where people live. Our apartment building is a **shelter** for my family. (page 104)

slavery When one person owns another person. **Slavery** is against the law in the United States. (page 168)

state Part of a country. Georgia is a **state** in the south part of our country. (page G7)

suburb A community just outside of a city. I live in a **suburb** of a large city. (page 18)

symbol Something that stands for something else. The flag is a **symbol** of our country. (page G5)

tax Money that people pay to the community. We pay **tax** money to our city for services. (page 123)

time line Shows the order in which things happen. Bob's **time line** shows when he started school. (page 130)

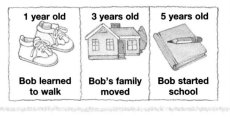

trade Sending goods to a country and getting others back from that country. We **trade** goods with Japan. (page 101)

tradition A special way of doing something that was passed down over time. A birthday cake with roses is a **tradition** in my family. (page 4)

transportation A way of moving people or goods. An airplane is a fast form of **transportation**. (page 20)

valley Low land between hills or mountains. Our town is in a **valley**. (page 55)

vote To choose something. Our class can **vote** on our class trip. (page 122)

wants Things people would like to have but do not need to live. This football and pair of skates are **wants**. (page 105)

White House Where the President lives and works. The **White House** is in Washington, D.C. (page 136)

index

CREDITS

Cover: Pentagram

Maps: Geosystems

Illustrations: Karen Bell: pp 212-213, 214, 215; Alex Bloch: pp 190-191, 192-193, 194-195; Nan Brooks: pp 104, 105, 108-109; Luisa DiAugusta: pp 12-13; Kathleen Dunne: pp 34, 35, 36, 74, 75, 82, 83, 84-85, 110, 112, 144, 145(t), 146, 182, 184, 216, 218; Franklin Hammond: pp 142-143; Meryl Henderson: pp 130, 131, 153; Mitch Hyatt: pp 3233; Susan Lexa: pp 76(b), R10-R17; Bonnie Matthews: pp 44-45, 110-111(border), 216-217; Karen Minot: pp R8-R9; Hima Pamoedjo: p 22, 23, 86, 87, 95, 96, 97, 160, 161, 217(t); Lisa Pomerants: pp 14-15, 16-17; Rebecca Perry: pp G5, 111(t), 183(t); Stacey Schuett: pp 144-145; Susan Swan: pp 23, 11, 38-39, 80-81, 116-117, 150-151, 188-189; Peggy Tagel: 9293; David Wenzel: pp 156, 157

Photography Credits: All photographs are by the McGraw-Hill School Division (MSD) except as noted below.

cover and i: Carol Gachupin (Lucero) Jemez Pueblo, NM/White Buffalo Gallery, photo by Bob Esparza for MMSD. iv: t. Doug Wilson/First Light; b. Lawrence Migdale/Photo Researchers. v: t. Doug Armand/Tony Stone Images; t.m. Robert Frerck/Odyssey, Chicago; b.m. The Bettmann Archive; b. Anthony Gruerio/Superstock. vi: Ken Karp for Daemmrich; m. Jack Wilburn/Animals Animals; t. Phil Degginger. G4: J. A. Kraulis/Masterfile.

29: t. Superstock. 37: t. Monica Stevenson for MMSD. Unit 2 38: m.l. Comstock/Cameron Davidson; b.r. Grant Heilman Photography; m.r. Dean Conger/National Geographic Society; t.l. David Muench. 39: m. Ron Watts/Westlight; t.l. Paul Conklin/Photo Edit.

47: t.l. Focus On Sports; m. Cary Wolinsky/Stock Boston. 50: m. Francis Westfield for MMSD; t. Adam Woolfitt/Woodfin Camp & Associates; b. Odyssey/Frerck, Chicago. 51: b. Guy Stubbs/Black Star; t. John Lei/Stock Boston, Inc.; m. Hiroyuki Matsumoto/Black Star. 52: b. H. Richard Johnson/FPG International. 53: t. Grant Heilman/Grant Heilman Photography, Inc.; b. Keith Gunar/Bruce Coleman, Inc. 54: t. David Muench Photography; b. Brian Bailey/ProFiles West. 55: t. Phil Schemreister/Tony Stone Images, Inc.; b. Paul Conklin/PhotoEdit. 56: t. Dean Conger/National Geographic Society; b. Comstock/Cameron Davidson. 58: t. Randy Wells/Tony Stone Images. 60: t. Greg Ferguson/Stock South. 61: t.r. Lee Snider/The Image Works; m.r. Robert Brenner/PhotoEdit; b.l. David Rosenberg/Tony Stone Images, Inc. 62: t.r. Doug Wilson/First Light; b. P.F. Bentley/Black Star. 64: Rob Nelson/Black Star. 64-65: Mike Dobel Masterfile. 65: Michelle Scott/Kids For A Clean Environment. 79: t. Monica Stevenson for MMSD. Unit 3: 80: b.r. Bryce Flynn/Stock Boston. 85: Curtis Martin. 88: l. Larry Lefever/Grant Heilman Photography, Inc.; r. Grant Heilman/Grant Heilman, Inc. 89: l. Grant Heilman Photography, Inc.; r. John Colwell/Grant Heilman Photography, Inc. 90: Grant Heilman Photography, Inc. 95: l. Alvis Upitis/The Image Bank; t.r. Pleasant/FPG International. 96: l. Oregon Department of Agriculture-Information Office; t.r. Del Monte. 97: John Zoiner. 98-99: Jeanne Drake/Tony Stone Worldwide. 99: t., b. Doug Plummer. 115: t. Monica Stevenson for MMSD. Unit 4 116: t.r. 92 John P. Endress/The Stock Market; m.l. Larry Lee/Westlight; m.r. Mark Reinstein, 1993/FPG International. 117: t. Joe Viesti/Viesti Associates, Inc.; b.l. Dennis OiClair/Tony Stone Worldwide. 119: b. Jim Stratford for MMSD. 121: Jim Stratford for MMSD. 123: Jim Stratford for MMSD. 128: b. Nawrocki Stock Photo, Inc. 129: l. Joe Flowers/Black Starr; r. Bettmann Archive. 132-133: Architect of the Capitol, Washington, D.C. 133: t. Dennis O'Clair/Tony Stone Worldwide. 139: Lawrence Migdale/Photo Researchers. 149: Monica Stevenson for MMSD. Unit 5 150: The Bettmann Archive. 151: t. Nanette Sanson/Superstock; m. Comstick; b. The Bettmann Archive. 152: Lawrence Migdale 154-155: Lawrence Migdale. 157: m. The Granger Collection. 162: Archive Photos. 163: l. Gary Andrashko; r. Arthur Gurmankin/Unicorn Stock Photos. 164: m. Archive Photos. 165: The Bettmann Archive. 166: MacMillan/McGraw-Hill files. 167-168. The Bettmann Archive. 169: l. The Granger Collection; r. Brown Brothers. 170-171: m. H. Armstrong Roberts. 171: t. Robert Frerck/Odyssey Chicago. 172: b.l. Martha Cooper/Viesti Associates; m.r. Robert Milazzo for MMSD; m.l. Miro Vintoniu/Stock Boston, Inc.; t.m. Bob Daemmrich/Stock Boston. 173: Jane Lidz/FStock, Inc. 174: t.l. Linda Schere. 174-175: Dennis MacDonald/Unicorn Stock Photos. 174-175: b. Ken Karp for MMSD. 175: t.r. Jim Shippee/Unicorn Stock Photos. 187: t. Monica Stevenson for MMSD. Unit 6 188: t. Stock Montage, Inc.; m.l. The Bettmann Archive; b. David Bartruff/FPG International; m.r. Joe Sohm/The Stock Market. 189: t. D. Dietrich/FPG International; m. Rob Schoenbaum/Black Star. 190: l. Museum of Fine Arts Boston; r. Archive Photos. 191: r. Bettmann Archive; l. Archive Photos. 192: l. Photoworld/FPG International. 198: b.r. David Noble/FPG International; b. Annie Griffiths Belt/Westlight; t. Peter Saloutos/Stock Market. 201: t. Comstock; t.l. Michael J. Howell/Picture Cube; t.m. Annie Griffiths Belt/Westlight; t.r. Comstock; m.l. David Noble/FPG International; m.r. C.C. Lockwood/D. Donne Bryant Stock Photography; b.l. Pete Saloutos/The Stock Market; b.m. TravelPix/FPG International; b.r. Nik Wheeler/Westlight. 204: b.l. Bachmann/Photo Researchers; b.r. Joseph Rodriguez/Black Star. 205: b.r. Lawrence Migdale/Photo Researchers; b.l. Comstock. 207: t.r. Pascal Quittemelle/Stock Boston; t.l., b.r. Monica Stevenson for MMSD; b.l. Joe viesti/Viesti Associates. 208: t.l. Joe Viesti/Viesti Associates; b.r. Robert Frerck/Odyssey Productions; t.r., b.l. Monica Stevenson for MMSD. 209: m.l. Joe Viesti/Viesti Associates; m.r. Monica Stevenson for MMSD. 212: Lisa Quinonens/Black Star. 213: The Granger Collection. 214: t.l. Anthony Gruerio/Superstock; t.m. Art Resource; t.r. The Bettmann Archive; b. Richard Vogel/Gamma Liaison. 215: Ed Pritchard/Tony Stone Images. 221: t. Monica Stevenson for MMSD. Endpapers: Bridgeman Art Library.

Additions:

2: t.l. ; t.m. Comstock; l.m. Weststock. 3: m. Tony Stone Images; r.m. Uniphoto; b.r. Ken Cavanagh for MMSD. 4: m. Lawrence Migdale for MMSD. 45: Ken Cavanagh for MMSD. 6: MMSD. 7: t. Ken Cavanagh for MMSD; b. Lawrence Migdale for MMSD. 8: t.l. Superstock; t.l. Photo Researchers; t.r. Superstock; t.r. Photo Researchers; m.l. Superstock; m.r. Woodfin Camp; m. Westlight. 9: t.l. Uniphoto; t.l. Superstock; t.r. Archive Photos; m.r. Wendy Weiss. Balance of photos Ken Cavanagh for MMSD.

10: b. Ken Cavanagh for MMSD. 11: t. Ken Cavanagh for MMSD; b. Uniphoto. 12: p/u from page 8. 13: p/u from page 9. 14: t. Bob Ortel; b. Photo Researchers/Renee Lynn. 15: t. Bob Ortel; b. Bob Ortel. 16: l. Bob Ortel; r. Bob Ortel. 17: Ken Cavanagh for MMSD; b. Weststock Charles Gurche. 18: t. Lawrence Migdale; b. Ken Cavanagh for MMSD.

19: t. Lawrence Migdale. 20: b.l. Vieste Winslow; b.r. MMSD. 21: t.l. Stock Boston/John Elk; t.r. Lawrence Migdale; b.r. pick/up. 24: t. Ken Cavanagh for MMSD. 25: t. Archive Photo. 26: Ken Cavanagh for MMSD. 27: t. Mark Guerra; b. Ken Cavanagh for MMSD. 28: b. Lawrence Migdale. 29: t. Lawrence Migdale. 84: m. ; b. ; (still waiting for photos to come back from Pub Works). 86: b. Tony Stone Images. 87: t. Ken Cavanagh for MMSD. 153: Lawrence Migdale. 154: t. Lawrence Migdale. 155: Lawrence Migdale.

(continued from page ii)

Acknowledgements

The book cover of **The Talking Cloth** by Rhonda Mitchell, Copyright ©1997, published by Orchard Books, is reprinted by permission of the publisher.
The book cover of **Celebrating Families** by Rosmarie Hausherr, Copyright © 1997, published by Scholastic Press, is used by permission of the publisher.
The book cover of **How My Parents Learned to Eat** by Ina R. Friedman, Copyright © 1984, published by Houghton Mifflin Company, is reprinted by permission of the publisher.
The book cover of **Nine O'Clock Lullaby** by Marilyn Singer, Copyright © 1991, published by HarperCollins, is reprinted by permission of the publisher.
The book cover of **Earthdance** by Joanne Ryder, Copyright © 1996, published by Henry Holt and Company, is reprinted by permission of the publisher.
The book cover of **How to Make an Apple Pie and See the World** by Marjorie Priceman, Copyright © 1994, published by Alfred A. Knopf, is reprinted by permission of the publisher.
The book cover of **A Fruit and Vegetable Man** by Roni Schotter, Copyright © 1993, published by Little, Brown and Co., is reprinted by permission of the publisher.
The book cover of **Ox-Cart Man** by Donald Hall, Copyright © 1979, published by Viking Press, is reprinted by permission of the publisher.
The book cover of **Arthur Meets the President** by Marc Brown, Copyright © 1991, published by Little, Brown and Co., is reprinted by permission of the publisher.
The book cover of **City Green** by DyAnne DiSalvo-Ryan, Copyright © 1994, published by Morrow Junior Books, is reprinted by permission of the publisher.
The book cover of **A Flag for Our Country** by Eve Spencer, Copyright © 1994, published by Steck-Vaughn, is reprinted by permission of the publisher.
The book cover of **Harriet Tubman and Black History Month** by Polly Carter, Copyright © 1990, published by Silver Burdett Press, Inc., is reprinted by permission of the publisher.
The book cover of **Watch the Stars Come Out** by Riki Levinson, Copyright © 1985, published by Dutton Books, is reprinted by permission of the publisher.
The book cover of **The Legend of the Blue Bonnet** by Tomie DePaola, Copyright © 1983, published by G. P. Putnam's Sons, is reprinted by permission of the publisher.
The book cover of **Lion Dancer: Ernie Wan's Chinese New Year** by Kate Waters and Madeline Slovenz-Low, Copyright © 1990, published by Scholastic Inc., is reprinted by permission of the publisher.
The book cover of **A Picture Book of George Washington** by David A. Adler, Copyright © 1989, published by Holiday House, is reprinted by permission of the publisher.
The book cover of **Hooray a Pinata!** by Elisa Kleven, Copyright © 1996, published by Dutton Children's Books, is reprinted by permission of the publisher.

The Princeton Review
—— Handbook of ——
Test-Taking Strategies

FILLING IN BUBBLES

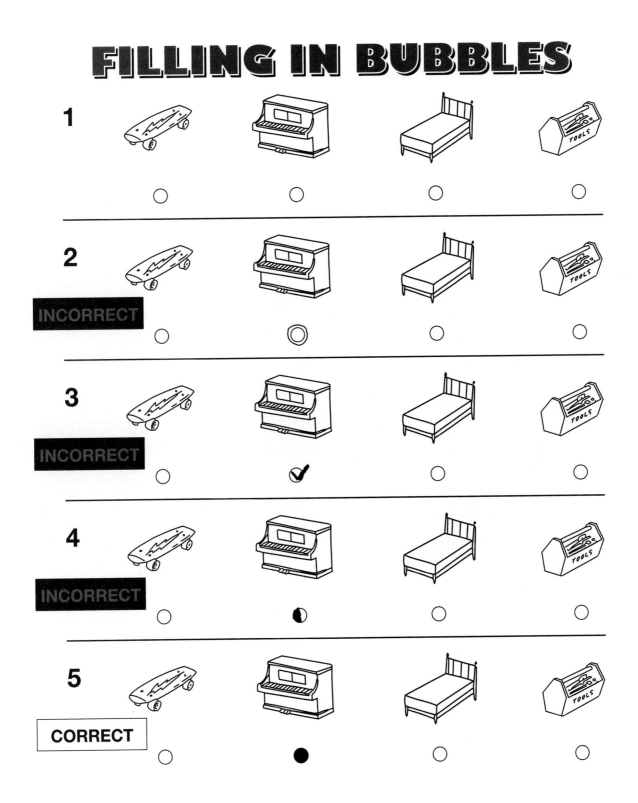

LISTEN CAREFULLY

			FEBRUARY			
Sunday	Monday	Tuesday	Wednesday	Thursday	Friday	Saturday
			1	2 Groundhog Day	3	4
5	6	7	8	9	10	11
12	13	14 Valentine's Day	15	16	17	18
19	20 Presidents' Day	21	22	23	24	25
26	27	28				

1 ○ Valentine's Day

○ Memorial Day

○ Groundhog Day

○ Presidents' Day

Remember: Do not write in your textbook.

NUMBERED ANSWERS

1

2

3

4

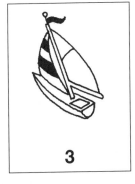

5

6

1

3 ○   4 ○   5 ○   6 ○

2

2 ○   3 ○   4 ○   5 ○

Remember: Do not write in your textbook.

READING A NEIGHBORHOOD MAP

This is a neighborhood map. It shows the route of the school bus from the school to Joe's house.

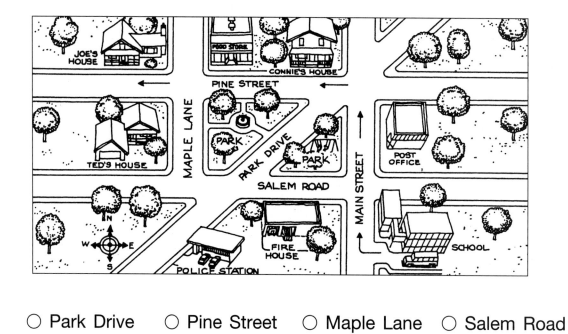

1   ○ Park Drive   ○ Pine Street   ○ Maple Lane   ○ Salem Road

2   ○ Maple Lane   ○ Main Street   ○ Pine Street   ○ Park Drive

Remember: Do not write in your textbook.

READING A MAP KEY

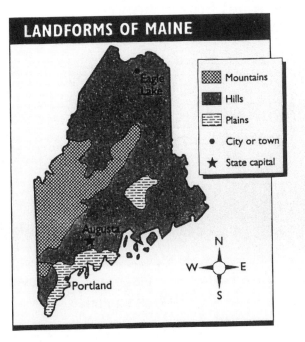

LANDFORMS OF MAINE

Key:
- Mountains
- Hills
- Plains
- • City or town
- ★ State capital

1 ○ Mountains

○ Plains

○ Ocean

○ Hills

Books Carl Found About Famous Americans

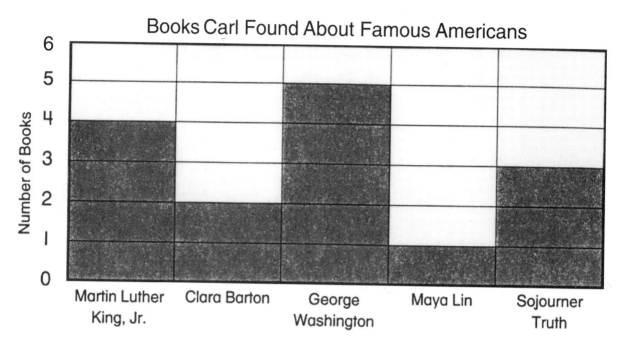

1 ○ Clara Barton

○ George Washington

○ Maya Lin

○ Martin Luther King, Jr.

Remember: Do not write in your textbook.

TELLING A REBUS STORY

1
1 ○ 2 ○ 4 ○ 5 ○

2
2 ○ 3 ○ 4 ○ 5 ○

Remember: Do not write in your textbook.

SHOWING WHAT YOU HAVE LEARNED

1 The low land between two hills or mountains is called a

- ○ plain
- ○ valley
- ○ island
- ○ peninsula

2 Martin Luther King, Jr., was a great

- ○ astronaut
- ○ President
- ○ leader
- ○ scientist

Remember: Do not write in your textbook.